THE
CHURCH
OF
CHRIST

THE
CHURCH
OF
CHRIST

THE DISTINCTIVE NATURE OF THE
NEW TESTAMENT CHURCH

EDWARD C. WHARTON

Gospel Advocate Company
1006 Elm Hill Pike
Nashville, Tennessee 37210

All Scripture quotations are from the New King James Version
unless otherwise noted.

Published by Gospel Advocate Co.
1006 Elm Hill Pike
Nashville, TN 37210
e-mail: gospeladv@aol.com

ISBN 0-89225-464-5

To my Mother, who taught me
to respect the Bible

TABLE OF CONTENTS

INTRODUCTION

The church of our Lord stands firmly established in the love and eternal purpose of God. In his letter to the Ephesians, Paul focuses on the pivotal role the church plays in the ongoing revelation of the eternal mystery and purpose of God; it is through the church that God has revealed this mystery to all. It is in the church that God and his purpose are glorified (Eph. 3:21). It is in the church, the one body of Christ, that God reconciles the world to himself through the cross of Jesus (Eph. 1:22, 23; 2:15, 16). It is in the church that we realize in the fullest degree the love of Christ, for Jesus "loved the church and gave himself up for her" (Eph. 5:25). One cannot understand God's eternal purpose and love without a deep appreciation for, and understanding of, the church. In fact, one cannot properly understand Jesus without a clear vision of the church, for the church and Jesus are one. The church is the body of Christ (Eph. 1:22, 23).

Ed Wharton's study of the church is an attempt to direct attention away from human denominational and sectarian understanding of the church, and to present the universal church, loved and established by Jesus. He challenges us to see the church for which Paul, like his Savior, gave his life in preaching "to the Gentiles the unsearchable riches of Christ" (Eph. 3:8).

I have known Ed Wharton for many years. I know of no one with a greater and more intense passion for preaching the mystery of Christ revealed in the church. He is totally committed to a restoration of the church as proposed by God and described in Scripture. He has a keen understanding of the unity and undenominational nature of the church and, like Paul, has given his life in proclaiming the simplicity and uniqueness of the church of our Lord. I commend this book to the reader as a study that challenges one to see beyond denominationalism and every sectarian spirit and to come to an appreciation of the unity of the church for which Jesus gave his life.

The clear message of this volume, calling for a return to a pure undenominational, non-sectarian understanding of the church, is worthy of our attention, especially in an age in which the church of our Lord faces serious challenges from within. If these challenges are not detected, they will further divide and fragment our ability to reach out effectively into all the world with the precious message of Jesus.

Ian Fair
Dean Emeritus
College of Biblical Studies
Abilene Christian University

PART ONE

THE DISTINCTIVE NATURE OF THE CHURCH

If all is form there can be no freedom, but equally, with no form the stress on freedom leads to anarchy and chaos.

Os Guinness, *The Dust of Death*, p. 92.

CHAPTER I

THE DISTINCTIVE PATTERN OF NEW TESTAMENT CHRISTIANITY

The Bible teaches that we are to glorify God "in the church by Christ Jesus throughout all ages, world without end" (Eph. 3:21). From the beginning the church has existed, not only in its nature as the saved body of Christ but also in a distinct form or structure in which she has been designed to function to the glory of God. Because of this unique nature and form, the church of Christ possesses distinctive marks of identity.

The intent of this lesson is to demonstrate that Christianity, and consequently the church, has been ordered after a divine plan and that God intended that plan to be the pattern by which the church in the New Testament can be identified and reproduced throughout history.

I. The Pattern Concept Defined

From the Greek, *tupos* means standard, pattern, form, figure and example. The biblical use of the term carries these ideas:

A. The Moral Idea

Christians whose lives are worthy of imitation are held up in Scripture as models or patterns of the Christian lifestyle. Paul said of the apostles, "Brethren, join in following my example, and note those who so walk, as you have us for a pattern" (Phil. 3:17). Evangelists are to be models for believers to imitate (1 Tim. 4:12; Titus 2:7).

B.   The Technical Sense

The word *tupos* is used of a "pattern in conformity to which a thing must be made,"[1] as when God commanded Moses to make the tabernacle "according to the pattern that he had seen" (Acts 7:44). The writer of Hebrews also speaks of God's instruction to Moses when he was about to make the tabernacle, "See that you make all things according to the pattern which was shown you in the mountain" (Heb. 8:5).

C.   The Doctrinal Sense

Tupos is used of a particular teaching. Paul reminded the Roman Christians that they had obeyed from the heart a form (*tupon*) of teaching in order to be made free from sin (Rom. 6:17-18). Paul charged Timothy to hold a distinct body of doctrine (teaching): "Hold the pattern of sound words which you have heard from me" (2 Tim. 1:13).

A pattern may be thought of as a mold, cast or form into which some substance such as concrete, lead or wax is poured, and each time the same image is reproduced. Doctrinally speaking the pattern concept should produce the idea of doctrinal identity. Consequently modern church builders should search the scripture for and attempt to conform to the same pattern of teaching that the apostles delivered to first-century churches. This pattern of teaching gives the church her distinct identity of nature and form.

II.   The Pattern Principle

The pattern principle means no more than going to the Bible to discover what God wants His people to believe, to be and to do until Jesus returns. The pattern embraces what men are to believe and do in order to be saved, it embraces the Christian lifestyle, it embraces certain elements of corporate worship in the church's assemblies as well as an individual's daily worship for God's Glory and our spiritual benefit, it embraces the work of the church and the organizational structure of both the universal church and of the local congregations. The pattern principle implies that what God revealed to the apostles to be preached, believed and obeyed in the apostolic age can be identified in the New Testament, and that God intentionally made that clear in New Testament writings so that this same message would be reproduced in proclamation and practice throughout history until Christ returns. The New Testament pattern principle insures the identity of the body of Christ as God purposed it from eternity.

Not only, then, was the church in the first century ordered after divine pattern, but the church throughout history is to be ordered after the same pattern to the extent of our ability to recognize and reproduce it (2 Tim. 2:2).

The following demonstrates that there is a pattern of teaching in the New Testament after which Christianity, and consequently the church, is to be ordered.

A.   The Eternal Purpose of God

Back of the church in the Bible and in history lies the eternal purpose of God. The Bible teaches that God's purpose in Christ for our salvation includes the church wherein we are to glorify him throughout history (Eph. 1:9-11; 3:10-11, 20-21). This purpose is referred to as the wisdom of God which he "ordained before the ages for our glory" (1 Cor. 2:7). From this purpose, as revealed in the New Testament, emerges the pattern of God's own making after which the apostolic church was originally constructed.

B.   The Apostles' Pattern

Jesus prayed for the unity of all who believe in him, saying, "I do not pray for these alone, but also for those who believe in me through their word; that they all may be one" (John 17:20-21). Clearly, the ground of belief in Christ and the unity of all believers is the word of his apostles. Their word, therefore, necessarily becomes the pattern of belief and resultant unity for all who would follow Christ. Consider these examples of the pattern principle:

1. Acts 2:42. In the beginning the church "continued steadfastly in the apostles' doctrine." Jesus' prayer for the unity of the church as based on the apostles' word is realized here at this earliest moment in the history of the church. The church had a distinctive teaching from the apostles and continued steadfastly in it. This same teaching was the pattern of instruction for the early church.

2. *1 Corinthians 4:17.* "For this reason I have sent Timothy to you, who is my beloved and faithful son in the Lord, who will remind you of my ways in Christ, as I teach everywhere in every church." Paul's teachings were to be maintained in perpetuity inasmuch as the preacher was to remind the churches of Paul's original teaching. Obviously the Holy Spirit intended the apostles' teaching to be the universal pattern of instruction since they taught the same thing among all the churches. That pattern of teaching constituted the basis of the early church's belief and consequent unity and identity.[3]

3. *1 Corinthians 7:17.* "And so I ordain in all the churches." In context there was a particular practice to which Paul directed all the churches. All the churches of Christ come under a common obligation to observe whatever apostolic authority directs. From this we perceive a pattern of teaching.

4. *1 Corinthians 14:34-37.* "Let the women keep silent in the churches. ... If anyone thinks himself to be a prophet or spiritual, let him acknowledge that the things which I write to you are the commandments of the Lord." A universal practice to be observed among the churches is clearly taught. Paul undergirds the importance of retaining the practice of women keeping silent in the assemblies by insisting that Christians acknowledge his writings as the very commandments of Christ.

Paul grounds this teaching not in cultural practice but in accordance with the law of Moses. In agreement with this exposition Paul also grounds this same instruction in the creation as he reveals God's original intent for men and women regarding particular areas of human activity from the beginning (1 Tim. 2:1-15).

5. *2 Timothy 2:2.* "And the things that you have heard from me among many witnesses, commit these to faithful men who will be able to teach others also." Paul's commission to Timothy to pass along his teaching to others who will pass it on to yet others is reminiscent of Christ's commission to the apostles to make disciples of all nations, "teaching them to observe all things that I have commanded you" (Matt. 28:19-20). The teachings of Christ through his apostles are to be passed along in perpetuity.

6. 1 John 4:1, 6. "Beloved, do not believe every spirit, but test the spirits, whether they are of God; because many false prophets have gone out into the world. ... We are of God; he who knows God hears us; he who is not of God does not hear us. By this we know the spirit of truth and the spirit of error." In this context the *spirits* seem to be different teachings, those that are different from the teachings of the Holy Spirit through the apostles. We are not told to test the teachers but their teachings. The standard for the test is the apostles' teachings. By comparison with their teachings we can know the truth or the error of another's doctrine.

"Pattern theology" is a term expressing the belief that the apostles' teachings for the first-century church are to be reproduced and observed until Jesus comes. By this means the uniqueness of the original Christian faith and the consequent unity of the body of Christ can be achieved and maintained not only in theory but also in reality.

C. The Apostles' Traditions

A tradition is that which is handed down. The Lord cautioned against traditions of men that invalidate the Word of God (Matt. 15:6). However, the traditions of the apostles, handed down from the Lord, are to be handed on to the church who is to hold them firmly.

1. What the apostles "received from the Lord" by revelation they "delivered" to the churches by inspiration (1 Cor. 11:23; 15:3).[4]

2. The churches are to hold firmly to the traditions taught by the apostles (1 Cor. 11:2; 15:1-2; 2 Thess. 2:15).

The apostles' teachings are equated with traditions. What the apostles received from Christ they handed on to the churches. The churches, in turn, were charged to hold the traditions they were taught whether by word or by the apostles' letters.

Hence the apostles' traditions constitute a pattern of teaching that is to be firmly held and passed on to future generations of the church until Christ returns.

D.   The Preacher's Charge

Paul urged Timothy to remain in Ephesus so that he might charge some to teach no other doctrine (1 Tim. 1:3). Observance of such instruction requires distinctiveness of doctrine to identify those who teach to the contrary. Paul passed on a similar admonition to the brethren at Rome when he directed them to "note those who cause divisions and offenses, contrary to the doctrine which you learned, and avoid them" (Rom. 16:17). There must be a divine standard against which doctrines can be tested for correctness; otherwise, doctrinal differences cannot be distinguished.

Paul's final instructions to the preacher include: "Hold fast the pattern of sound words which you have heard from me, in faith and love which are in Christ Jesus" (2 Tim. 1:13). The word "pattern" is rendered "standard" in the NASB: "Retain the standard of sound words." The NIV also renders "pattern": "What you heard from me, keep as the pattern of sound teaching."

Within the apostles' teachings lies a pattern of instruction for the church. And God expects his church to *hold* it, *retain* it, *keep* it.

The Bible teaches specific doctrines such as, the inspiration of Scripture, the deity of Christ, the atonement, the gospel of justification by grace through faith in Christ, baptism, the nature of the church, the organization of the church, the work of the church, the Christian lifestyle, worship, the Lord's Supper, the Second Coming, the Resurrection, the final judgment, eternal life and eternal condemnation. From such teachings emerge the pattern of sound words that is to be reproduced and lived by the Lord's church until Jesus comes.

E.   The Faith

When the New Testament speaks of "the faith," it refers to the thing believed rather than the act of believing. The

Christian religion as a system of justification by faith in Christ is therefore often referred to as "the faith" and is presented in the New Testament as both *singular* (one) and *distinctive* (identifiable). Paul tells us there is but one faith (Eph. 4:4-5) and that Christians can "all come to the unity of the faith" (v. 13). This requires a doctrinal identity in order to distinguish the faith from counterfeits.

Religious unity requires unity of belief. Notice the New Testament's emphasis on the singularity of the faith. It is *the* faith. *The* faith can be preached (Gal. 1:23), obeyed (Acts 6:7), and continued in (Acts 14:22). We are to strive for *the* faith (Phil. 1:27), and contend for *the* faith (Jude 3). We can deny *the* faith (1 Tim. 5:8); we can go astray from *the* faith (1 Tim. 6:21). In each case it is *the* faith. The apostles do not teach us to negotiate a unity between conflicting beliefs. Rather we are all to seek *the* unity of *the* faith. One is not speaking biblically when he speaks of different faiths of the Christian religion.

Christian unity can be achieved and maintained only when we believe and admit that the faith is absolute (there is but *one* faith) (Eph. 4:4-5) and attainable (we are *all* to come to the unity of the faith) (Eph. 4:11-13). As students of God's Word, we may not agree on every point, but as believers in Christ we are to try to determine from Scripture what constitutes the faith. Then in the spirit of patience and humility, forbearing one another in love, we should strive to unify upon that one faith revealed in the New Testament.

F.   The Truth

Jesus said, "If you abide in my word you are my disciples indeed. And you shall know the truth and the truth shall make you free" (John 8:31-32). In context (vv. 31-36) Jesus is speaking about the truth of his word that makes us free from sin. This "truth" is a distinct body of truth. Jesus says we can "know" that truth. Peter speaks about this same body of truth purifying our souls at the time we "obey" it (1 Peter 1:22). Jesus said his truth would make us free from sin. Peter tells us our souls will be purified from sin when we *obey* that truth. Inherent in this language is a distinct body of truth for alien sinners. It can be known and obeyed and will result in purifying the sinner's soul from sin.

G. The Word of God Is Like Seed

When Jesus relates the parable of the sower, he speaks about seed falling onto different kinds of soils, which he likens to the hearts of men (Luke 8:4-15). He then says, "The seed is the word of God" (v. 11). We know that seed brings forth after its kind (cf. Gen. 1:11-12). Never have apple seeds brought forth oranges or potatoes. Without exception we can rely on God's Word to bring forth Christians. It will produce a New Testament church in this modern era. We must admit that the pure Word of God, unmixed by human wisdom, will bring forth the church of Christ as it did in the first century.

III. Conclusion

Scripture reveals that Christianity is ordered after a divine pattern and that it therefore possesses a distinct identity. Christianity was designed by the Lord and preached by the apostles. The early church was taught to hold the pattern of their words. Based on the pattern principle, the church of Jesus Christ can be identified in the New Testament and is intended to be reproduced in perpetuity until Jesus comes.

Quick-Answer Questions

1. Does the New Testament teach that Christianity is ordered after a pattern?
2. Can New Testament Christianity be identified?
3. If Christianity is distinctive, can error be identified?
4. Define traditions (1 Cor. 11:23).
5. Does the New Testament ask the church to hold some traditions? If so, which ones (1 Cor. 11:2 and 2 Thess. 2:15)?
6. Do you believe the New Testament teaches that the apostles' teachings are to be taught in perpetuity until Jesus comes?
7. Do you believe the term "pattern theology" expresses a New Testament idea?

Discussion Questions

1. Explain how Scriptures like 1 Corinthians 4:17 and 2 Timothy 1:13 undergird the concept of pattern theology. Do you think denominationalism could survive where these Scriptures are applied? Why or why not?

2. Relate whether the church could be identified in Scripture or reproduced today without a pattern of teaching concerning the church.

3. Discuss what is meant by the nature, form and function of the church.

4. Beginning with 2 Timothy 2:2, discuss whether God has designed the church to believe, be and do certain things in perpetuity.

5. John said the church can know the difference between truth and error. Explain from 1 John 4:1-6 how this is to be achieved.

6. Examine what Jesus said is the basis for Christian unity according to John 17:20-21, and what Paul referred to as the basis for unity in Ephesians 4:13. Discuss whether there is a basic difference or an agreement between them.

7. Discuss whether the teachings and practice of denominationalism are in agreement with, or are departures from, the apostles' teachings in Ephesians 4:4-6, 11-13, and 2 Timothy 2:2 regarding the pattern principle and the consequent unity of the body of Christ.

CHAPTER 2

THE DISTINCTIVE NATURE OF THE NEW COVENANT

Among God's provisions for man's redemption is the New Covenant of Christ. God's people are covenant people. They have entered into a covenant relationship with God in order to receive salvation.

A covenant is an agreement between participants. Covenants may be unconditional, as between God and Abram (Gen. 15:12-21), or conditional, as between God and Abraham and Abraham's offspring (Gen. 17:1-14) or between God and the nation of Israel (Ex. 19:1-5; Deut. 29:1, 9).

This lesson will be concerned with two conditional covenants: the law of Moses, called the Old Covenant (2 Cor. 3:14; Heb. 8:13), under which Israel existed as a theocratic nation, and the New Covenant of Christ. The Old Covenant was an agreement between God and the nation of Israel. The New Covenant is an agreement between Christ and individuals who constitute the church.

The intent of this lesson is to show that the church of Christ, God's covenant people, can be identified by the conditions required for salvation under the New Covenant.

I. The Passing of the Old Covenant

Much religious error is traceable to the failure to make a distinction between the Old and New Covenants.

A. The Old Covenant and the Law Are the Same

Exodus 24:1-8 records the dedication of the Old Covenant that contained "all the words which the Lord has said" in Exodus 20:1-23:33. This included the Ten Commandments (Ex. 20:1-17). The book of Hebrews speaks of this event referring to the Old Covenant as "the law" (Heb. 9:18-20). Therefore the Old Covenant and the law are the same.

B. The Old Covenant Removed

Since the Old Covenant and the Law are the same, what happens to one happens to the other.

1. The Mosaic Covenant became old and was ready to give way to the new. The book of Hebrews records that when Jeremiah predicted the coming of a New Covenant (Jer. 31:31-34), the Mosaic Covenant became old: "In that he says, 'A new Covenant,' he has made the first obsolete. Now what is becoming obsolete and growing old is ready to vanish away" (Heb. 8:13). Therefore the law of Moses, becoming old in Jeremiah's time, could not last indefinitely. At the cross the Old Covenant vanished, and the New was established (Heb. 8:6).[5]

2. The passing of the Old Covenant at the cross.

a. The old annulled to bring in the new (Matt. 26:28; Heb. 7:18-25). When Jesus died, it was to bring us the New Covenant for the remission of sins. But we could not draw near to God through that New Covenant until the first covenant was annulled. Then the New Covenant, called a "better hope," was brought in (Heb. 7:18-19).

Sometimes the writer of Hebrews uses a literary style called "the historical present" wherein a past event is referred to as if it is presently taking place. That is, "For on the one hand *there is* an annulling of the former commandment ... on the other hand, *there is* a bringing in of a better hope, through which we draw near to God" (Heb 7:18-19). This does not teach that at the time of the writing of Hebrews the "former commandment," the Old Law, was only in the process of being annulled or that the "better hope," the New Covenant, was not yet completely brought in. It is conclusive that at that time Christians were already drawing near to God (Heb. 7:25). Therefore, the Old Covenant had already been annulled, and the New Covenant had already been fully brought in by which they drew near to God.

b. *Delivered from the law to be joined to Christ (Rom. 7:4-7).* Paul wrote that Jewish Christians "have become dead to the law through the body of Christ ... we have been delivered from the law." He then points out that the law from which they had been delivered was the law that said, "You shall not covet." That, of course, was the 10th commandment. Clearly the Old Law had already passed by the time Paul wrote Romans.

c. *The Old Covenant done away in Christ (2 Cor. 3:3-14).* Paul says that the apostles were ministers of a New Covenant that stands in great contrast to the Old Covenant. He calls the Old Covenant "the letter that kills" that was "written and engraved on stones." He taught that just as the veil hid the radiance of Moses' face he acquired while in the presence of God when he received the tablets of stone, so also unbelieving Jews could not see the passing of the Old Covenant because of their hardened hearts that veiled their understanding.

d. *No longer under the law (Gal. 3:24-25).* Paul saw the law of Moses as analogous to a "tutor to bring us to Christ, that we might be justified by faith." Then he explains, "But after faith has come, we are no longer under a tutor." With the coming of the Christian faith, the law passed.

e. *The law abolished (Eph. 2:14-15).* Paul says "the law of commandments contained in ordinances" had been abolished in Christ's flesh, that is, by his crucifixion.

f. *The law nailed to the cross (Col. 2:13-14).* The Bible teaches that our trespasses have been forgiven since the Lord "wiped out the handwriting of requirements that was against us, which was contrary to us. And he has taken it out of the way, having nailed it to the cross." The handwriting of requirements, the law of Moses, which as a legal system held our sins against us, is analogous to the "bond" of ancient times and is similar to our I.O.U.

The bond was a written agreement recording the amount one borrowed. It was held against the borrower until the debt was paid. When paid the debt was canceled. The ink used in ancient times had no acid in it. Rather than take a bite out of the writing material, the ink dried on top and was easily erased or wiped out with a sponge or cloth. At the cross Jesus abolished the law which held our sins against us and thus figuratively wiped the slate clean, abolishing even the record of our sin debt.

g. *A change of priesthood requires a change of law (Heb. 7:11-12,19; 10:1).* The Old Law could perfect no one. But with the change in priesthoods from Levitical to Melchizedekian and with the ensuing necessity to change laws, God brought to us the New Covenant by which he can perfect us forever (Heb. 10:14; 13:20).

h. *The establishing of the second requires the removal of the first (Heb. 10:1-10).* This passage contrasts the sacrificial system of both covenants and stresses that the blood of animal sacrifices under the law can never take away sins. This shows the necessity of Christ's superior sacrifice in order to sanctify us from sin. Then it says, " 'Behold, I have come to do your will, O God.' He takes away the first (sacrificial system) that he may establish the second." The writer teaches that "through the offering of the body of Jesus Christ" at the cross the Old Law with its sacrificial system passed, and the new was brought in. Christ did the will of God consummating his work at the cross. Then the writer concludes, "By that will we have been sanctified."

It is conclusive that the Law of Moses, the Old Covenant, with its Sabbaths, circumcision and animal sacrifices, has been abolished, done away with at the cross. Such was essential for remission of sins to be offered under the New Covenant. It became old in the days of Jeremiah and vanished at Calvary. Redemption can be obtained only by observing the conditions of faith in Christ under the New Covenant.

II. The Promise of a New Covenant

Read carefully God's promise of the New Covenant as foretold by Jeremiah and the inspired quotation of the promise in the book of Hebrews:

The Prophecy:

Behold, the days are coming says, the Lord, when I will make a new covenant with the house of Israel and with the house of Judah – not according to the covenant that I made with their fathers in the day that I took them by the hand to bring them out of the land of Egypt, My covenant which they broke, though I was a husband to them, says the Lord. But this is the covenant I will make with the house of Israel after those days, says the Lord: I will put my law in their minds, and write it on their hearts; and I will be their God, and they shall be my people. No more shall every man teach his neighbor, and every man his brother, saying, 'Know the Lord,' for they all shall know me, from the least of them to the greatest of them, says the Lord. For I will forgive their iniquity, and their sin I will remember no more (Jer. 31:31-34).

The New Testament Quotation:

Behold, the days are coming, says the Lord, when I will make a new covenant with the house of Israel and with the house of Judah- not according to the covenant that I made with their fathers in the day when I took them by the hand to lead them out of the land of Egypt; because they did not continue in my covenant, and I disregarded them, says the Lord. For this is the covenant that I will make with the house of Israel after those days, says the Lord: I will put my laws in their mind and write them on their hearts; and I will be their God, and they shall be my people. None of them shall teach his neighbor, and none his brother, saying, Know the Lord, for all shall know me, from the least of them to the greatest of them. For I will be merciful to their unrighteousness, and their sins and their lawless deeds I will remember no more (Heb. 8:8-12).

A.   The Distinctive Nature of the New Covenant

Jeremiah's language points to the distinctive laws of the New Covenant by which God's people are identified and by which they have forgiveness of sins.

1. The New Covenant is different from the Old Covenant. Jeremiah specified the New Covenant would not be according to the one made with Israel when they came out from Egypt. Consider the differences.

2. Sins forgiven and forgotten under the New Covenant. The old law could not provide remission of sins (Acts 13:38-39; Gal. 2:16; 3:11). While forgiveness was provided for those *under* the law, it was not provided *by* that law. Make the distinction between the Old Testament as a revelation from God recording God's communication to Israel and those statements in the Old Testament that are terms of the Old Covenant. Forgiveness of sins was provided by faith in God (cf. Luke 18:9-14; Rom. 4:1-8).[6] But their sins were remembered in the annual sacrifices of the old sacrificial system (Heb. 10:1-4). Under the New Covenant there is forgiveness of sins, and they will not be remembered.

3. All shall know the Lord. Under the Old Covenant, God's people did not know him at the time they entered into covenant relationship with him. This was because of an earlier covenant God made with Abraham and all his offspring to be their God (Gen. 17:1-14). Hebrew children were born into a covenant relationship with God because of the covenant God had made with them while they were yet in the loins of Abraham. The covenant of circumcision for the male children on the eighth day was a sign or token of their covenant relationship with God as his children (Gen. 17:9-11). The Hebrews entered into covenant relationship with God at birth but for obvious reasons did not know it. Then as they grew up, they were taught to know the Lord and their special relationship with him. Under the New Covenant, without exception says Jeremiah, all who are in a covenant relationship with God will know it.

a. Jeremiah prophesied salvation by education under the New Covenant. The Lord said, "I will put my law in their minds." Then he adds, "They shall all know me, from the least of them to the greatest of them." Those under the New Covenant all know the Lord because they have been educated to Christ and the laws of the New Covenant. Laws are placed on men's minds by education. When men are taught the gospel, believe on Christ as Lord, and are educated to the laws and terms of the New Covenant for salvation and obey those laws, they become covenant related children of God and know it.

It is these of whom God said, "For I will forgive *their* iniquity, and *their* sin will I remember no more." Whose sins will be forgiven? Those who *know* the Lord by education to the gospel and the New Covenant. It is impossible to be a covenant-related child of God today and not know it. Hence, Jeremiah foretold salvation would be by education.

b. Jesus and the apostles taught salvation by education. After Jesus announced the great invitation, "Come to me, all you who labor and are heavy laden" (Matt. 11:28), he then stated the conditions by which "all" would come to him. He said no man can come to him unless God draws him. He then explained that God draws men to Christ just as it is written in the prophets: "And they shall all be taught by God. Therefore everyone who has heard and learned from the Father comes to me" (John 6:44-45). Jesus says that God draws men to Christ by the process of education, just as the prophets foretold. Those who hear are the ones who learn how to come to Christ. This is how God puts the laws of the New Covenant in our minds and hearts.

Salvation by education is what Jesus taught in the Great Commission (Matt. 28:18-20; Mark 16:15-16). Only men who are discipled by gospel teaching and thus brought to faith in Christ are to be baptized for salvation.

Paul taught salvation by education when he said we are saved by faith in Christ which comes by hearing the word of Christ (Rom. 5:1; 10:17).

B. The Identity of God's People

The Lord continues, "I will put my law in their minds,

and write it on their hearts." Then he says of these who are educated to the laws of his New Covenant, "And I will be THEIR God, and THEY shall be my people." We can know who God's people are today. They can be identified by whom they know and what they know: Christ, the gospel and the laws of pardon under the New Covenant.

Inherent in the term "law" is the idea of obedience. When one learns about Christ and the laws of the New Covenant for forgiveness of sins and obeys those laws from the heart, he becomes a covenant-related child of God. All who know the gospel and the laws of the New Covenant can identify God's people. These people are the ones of whom God says, "I will forgive their iniquity, and their sin I will remember no more." God's people are the ones forgiven. No one can lawfully lay claim to the Lord as his God until he has learned and obeyed the laws of Christ's New Covenant.

III. The Establishment of the New Covenant for Remission of Sins

As a legal system the old law required sinless perfection (Lev. 18:5; Gal. 3:12) and condemned the violator at the first infraction (Deut. 27:26; Gal. 3:10) but could not offer justification (Hab. 2:4; Gal. 3:11). Faith in God has been the principle of justification from the beginning (Gal. 3:6-9), and because "the law is not of faith" (Gal. 3:12), it was not in its nature to justify. This accounts for Paul's statement that "you could not be justified by the law of Moses" (Acts 13:38-39), hence the need for the New Covenant by which God provides forgiveness of sins.

A. The New Covenant Established on Better Promises of Forgiveness of Sins (Heb. 8:6-12)

The New Covenant promises and provides what the Old Covenant could not give and was "established" upon those "better promises" of forgiveness of sins for both our sake and the sakes of those who lived by faith under the old economy (Heb. 9:15). Jesus' death not only mediated the New Covenant but also provided remission of sins for those "under the first covenant." It was established for us and them (Heb. 11:40).

B. The New Covenant and Christ's Blood

At the Passover Jesus said of the cup, "This is my blood of the new covenant, which is shed for many for the remission of sins" (Matt. 26:28). As high priest, Jesus offered himself unto God as a sin offering. Then he took his own blood "into heaven itself, now to appear in the presence of God for us" (Heb. 9:11-24). In this context it is said, "without shedding of blood there is no remission" (Heb. 9:22). But Jeremiah said God gave the New Covenant for the forgiveness of sins. Thus the blood of Christ cannot be separated from obedience to the laws of the New Covenant as conditions to receive the remission of sins.

John says we are washed from our sins by his blood (Rev. 1:5). But Saul of Tarsus was commanded, "Arise and be baptized, and wash away your sins, calling on the name of the Lord" (Acts 22:16). Obviously, we are washed by the blood of Christ when baptized.

C. The New Covenant: The Means of Our Sanctification

1. We are sanctified by the blood of Christ (Heb. 9:13-14; 10:29). But we are sanctified when we obey the laws of the New Covenant (Heb. 10:14-17). Therefore we are sanctified by the blood of Christ when we obey the terms of the New Covenant.

2. We are sanctified by faith in Christ (Acts 26:18). But we are sanctified by obedience to the laws of the New Covenant (Heb. 10:14-17). Therefore we are sanctified when our faith in Christ leads us to obey the laws of the New Covenant.

D. The New Covenant: The New and Living Way (Heb. 10:19-20)

According to Hebrews, we enter into the holy place, that is, heaven (Heb. 9:24), not only by the blood of Christ, but also "by a new and living way which he consecrated for us."

But the "way" which he consecrated or dedicated is the New Covenant (Heb. 9:18-20). We, therefore, enter into heaven by the blood, which is shed for remission of our sins, *and* by the New Covenant, which is consecrated by his blood at his death. Both God's grace in Christ and man's obedience of faith are essential to obtain entrance into the eternal inheritance.

E. Laws of the New Covenant for Remission of Sins

Jeremiah said that the laws of the New Covenant must be in men's minds and hearts and that God would forgive their sins. Inherent in the term "law" is the idea of obedience. Whatever the New Testament teaches men to do to receive forgiveness of sins must, therefore, be the laws of the New Covenant to obey from the heart for forgiveness.

1. Faith is a law of the New Covenant. We are saved by faith in Christ (Rom. 5:1; Gal. 2:16; 3:26), but we are saved by obedience to the laws of the New Covenant (Heb. 10:14-17). Therefore, we must believe on Christ for remission of sins.

2. Baptism is a law of the New Covenant. Jeremiah promised that those who had the laws of the New Covenant in their minds and hearts would have forgiveness of sins. But on Pentecost, Peter commanded those who crucified Christ to "repent, and let every one of you be baptized in the name of Jesus Christ for the remission of sins" (Acts 2:38). The laws of the New Covenant are for remission of sins, but baptism is for remission of sin. Therefore baptism is a law of the New Covenant for remission of sins.

IV. The New Covenant and the Thief on the Cross

When Jesus said to the thief on the cross, "Assuredly, I say to you, today you will be with me in paradise" (Luke 23:43), it is conclusive that the thief was saved. But some assume that the thief was saved without being baptized and therefore baptism is not essential to our salvation under the New Covenant. Consider the following statements.

A. It Cannot Be Proven That the Thief Was Not Baptized

To say the thief was not baptized is an assumption without biblical foundation. The thief was commanded to be baptized for remission of sins under John the Baptist (Mark 1:4; Matt. 3:5-6; Luke 7:30). The only time the Bible mentions the thief is at his crucifixion with Christ (Luke 23:39-42). To say he was or was not baptized is to say what the Bible does not say. That he could have been baptized by John is, however, a distinct possibility.

B. The Thief and the Old and New Covenants

The difference between the salvation of the thief on the cross and the salvation of men today is the difference between living under the Old Covenant and living under the New Covenant. The thief was responsible for living under the Old Covenant while we today are under the New. The book of Hebrews makes it clear that "where there is testament, there must also of necessity be the death of the testator. For a testament is of force after men are dead, since it has no power at all while the testator lives" (9:16-17). The New Covenant was, therefore, not in force until after Jesus died, and its terms were not made known until the Day of Pentecost 53 days later. It was only after the thief died and Christ was raised that Jesus gave the universal command to be baptized in his name (Mark 16:15-16; Acts 2:38). The thief lived and died under the Old Covenant. He, therefore, never came under the command to be baptized in Jesus' name. We today come under that command.

The question as to whether the thief was baptized is thus seen to be of no consequence in relation to baptism for salvation.

C. The Thief Was Never Commanded to Be Baptized for New Covenant Reasons.

The New Testament clarifies the authority and various purposes of New Covenant baptism which are distinct from John's baptism.

1. Into the name of the Father, the Son, and the Holy Spirit (Matt. 28:19). In the original language this particular phrase, *eis to onoma*, means "into the possession of." [7] John's baptism was not for this purpose. Jews were born into covenant relationship with God and had no need to be baptized into covenant possession as we do today.

2. In the name of Jesus Christ (Acts 2:38). The original language for "in the name of" is *epi to onomati*. It is distinct from Matthew 28:19 (*eis to onoma*), and means "on the basis of" or "by the authority of." Peter pointed to the resurrection of Jesus as proof that Jesus was both Lord and Christ (Acts 2:36). It was on the basis of Jesus' authority as Lord that baptism was commanded in his name for remission of sins. The thief never heard this.

3. To receive the gift of the Holy Spirit (Acts 2:38). The indwelling gift of the Holy Spirit was not made available until Pentecost, 53 days after Jesus' death.

4. Into Christ's death (Rom. 6:3-4). Christ had not yet died when he saved the thief.

5. Into Christ's body, the church (1 Cor. 12:13). The church had not yet been established.

It should become apparent that all reasoning opposed to the necessity of New Covenant baptism which is based on the salvation of the thief on the cross is anachronistic in nature and, therefore, without subject relevance or scriptural substance.

B. What John's Baptism Was Not

While John's baptism was "a baptism for the remission of sins" (Mark 1:4), as in New Covenant baptism, it was not the "one baptism" of Ephesians 4:4-5. In contrast notice what John's baptism was not.

1. It was not to become the new possession of the new King (as with Christ's baptism, Matt. 28:19).

2. It was not a baptism into the covenant relationship with God as Father and with Christ and the Holy Spirit (Matt. 28:19).

3. It was not for all men (as in Matt. 28:19; Mark 16:15-

16); it was confined to covenant Jews.

4. It was not "in the name of Jesus Christ," i.e. authorized by Christ's new authority (as in Matt. 28:18-19; Acts 2:38).

5. It was not for renewing the old man by the Holy Spirit, to make a new man in Christ (as in Titus 3:4-5; cf Eph. 2:15).

6. It was not to receive the indwelling gift of the Holy Spirit (as in Acts 2:38; 5:32; Gal. 3:26-27; 4:6).

7. It was not into Christ and into his death (as in Rom. 6:3-4).

8. It was not to die to sin, to be raised and regenerated with "newness of life" (as in Rom. 6:3-4).

9. It was not to be united with Christ (as in Rom. 6:5).

10. It was not to crucify the old man, that the body of sin might be done away (as in Rom. 6:6).

11. It was not that we might be freed of the guilt and consequences of our future sins (as in Rom. 6:7).

12. It was not for entrance into the new blood-bought body of Christ (as in 1 Cor. 12:13).

13. It was not for redemption of the body (as in 1 Cor. 15:29; cf. Rom. 8:10). The body dies because of our sin , but Christ has redeemed our bodies which we will receive in glory at the resurrection (1 Cor. 6:13-20; 15:35-58).

14. It was not to be clothed with Christ (as in Gal. 3:26-27).

15. It was not an expression of faith in Christ to receive the Holy Spirit (as in Acts 19:1-5).

16. It was not an expression of faith in God to raise up our bodies from the dead as he raised up Christ (as in Col. 2:11-12).

17. It was not to be saved (as in 1 Peter 3:21).

18. It was not New Covenant baptism.

John's baptism was Old Covenant baptism, "For all the prophets and the law prophesied until John" (Matt. 11:13).[8] John's baptism was not the "one baptism" of the present New Covenant. Whether the thief on the cross may or may not have been baptized is of no consequence to those of us who live within the time frame of the New Covenant. Christ never commanded the thief to receive New Covenant baptism, but we have been commanded today.

IV. Conclusion

God's promise of a New Covenant for remission of sins has been fulfilled in the cross of Christ. The Old Covenant passed, and the New Covenant has been established on the better promises. All who place their faith in Christ and obey the conditions of pardon and fellowship are saved and become covenant related children of God. Since the church is the body of the saved, it is to be identified by the conditions (laws) of obedience required by the New Covenant for salvation.

Quick-Answer Questions

1. The Old Covenant was holy, just and good (Rom. 7:12). Why, then, was it called a ministration of condemnation (cf. 2 Cor. 3:7, 9)?
2. The Old Covenant was perfect as a legal system (Ps. 19:7). Why, then, was it taken away? (See Gal. 2:21; 3:11-12.)
3. Could the New Covenant and the Old Covenant run concurrently? (See Romans 7:4; Hebrews 7:12, 18-19.)
4. When did the Old Covenant become old (cf. Heb. 8:13)? When did the Old Covenant vanish away (cf. Heb. 8:8, 13)?
5. Was the Old Covenant abolished (Eph. 2:14-15)? When (cf. Heb. 10:5-10)?
6. If the old commandment was annulled at the cross, could the "better hope" have been brought in (cf. Heb. 7:18-19)?
7. In light of the above, what shall we conclude about the teaching that the law was not taken away until A.D. 70?

Discussion Questions

1. We have teachers in the New Covenant church (Acts 13:1; James 3:1). What did Jeremiah mean when he said that under the New Covenant, "No more shall every man teach

his neighbor" (Jer. 31:34)? Does this mean there will be no more need for teachers under the New Covenant?

2. Explain from the content of Jeremiah 31:33-34 and Hebrews 8:10-11 why God's people will all know him. Can a person be a child of God and not know it? Can a person be saved at baptism without knowing it?

3. Explain from Jeremiah 31:33-34 how God's people are to be identified, how the forgiven are to be identified.

4. Explain how the church of Christ is covenant-related to God.

5. We are saved by faith in Christ. Yet we must obey the laws of the New Covenant to be saved. Define saving faith; then explain the relation of the New Covenant to saving faith.

6. Was the thief on the cross saved without baptism? Does it make any difference to our salvation one way or the other? Explain from Hebrews 9:16-17.

7. If the New Covenant is for remission of sins (Jer. 31:34) and if baptism is for remission of sins (Acts 2:38), does that make baptism a law of Jeremiah 31:33? Explain.

CHAPTER 3

THE DISTINCTIVE IDENTITY OF THE NEW TESTAMENT CHURCH

The church of Christ has a distinctive nature by which it can be identified and reproduced throughout history. The purpose of this lesson is to define biblically the church and its distinctive identity.

I.   Definition and Use of the Word "Church"

From the Greek *ekklesia* comes our English words "church" and "assembly." It is a compound word from *ek* meaning "out of" and *klesis*, "a calling." The church is a called out body of people that belong to the Lord. He has called them out of one realm and into another.

A.   To the Greeks

In New Testament times the Greeks used *ekklesia* to refer to a lawful political body. The term was used in this manner by the Grecian city clerk at Ephesus where it is translated "assembly" in Acts 19:39. It is also used of a gathering of craftsmen at Ephesus who became riotous, where once again it is translated "assembly" (Acts 19:32, 41). *Ekklesia* thus embraced the idea of an assembled group of people who were called out of one realm, like homes and places of business, into another.

B.   In the New Testament

Ekklesia is translated by the word "church" where it refers to the saved body of Christ (Acts 2:47; 20:28; 1 Cor. 10:32; 1

Tim. 3:15). This redemptive meaning is behind the Lord's statement: "Upon this rock I will build my church" (Matt. 16:18). He builds his church by calling us out of sin to himself and by saving those who believe on him as Lord and respond to his call. Christ calls us by the gospel (2 Thess. 2:14; Acts 2:39). He calls us out of the darkness of ignorance into his wonderful light (1 Peter 2:9), into his own kingdom and glory (1 Thess 2:12). He calls us to be holy, sanctified, set apart from the world (1 Cor. 1:1-2). Those who hear the call and answer the call by an obedience of faith become the called out body of Christ. This saved body is his church, his body of believers that he called and saved out of sin.

C. Use of the Word Church in the Universal and Local Senses

1. The universal church. The church of Christ is the worldwide body of the saved. The New Testament uses the word "church" in this universal sense (e.g., Matt. 16:18; 1 Cor. 10:32; Eph. 1:22-23; 5:23, 25, 32; 1 Tim. 3:15). When men are saved, they are added to the universal church (Acts 2:47); they are "baptized into one body" (1 Cor. 12:13); they are reconciled in this one body (Eph. 2:16). On this basis, when we speak about the church of Christ, we should not think of a name but of a designation of relationship: the church that belongs to Christ.

2. The local church. There is also a more geographically restricted use of the word. It is used of an organized congregation of Christians in a particular locale, such as "the church that was at Antioch" (Acts 13:1), the church at Ephesus (Acts 20:17), "the church of God which is at Corinth" (1 Cor. 1:2), and "the church of the Thessalonians in God the Father and the Lord Jesus Christ" (1 Thess. 1:1). These are local churches. The New Testament speaks of the "the churches of Asia" (1 Cor. 16:19), "the churches of Galatia" (Gal. 1:2), and "the churches of Judea" (Gal. 1:22). They are the organized bodies of the universal church in different locales throughout the world. Paul indicated local churches when he said, "The churches of Christ greet you" (Rom. 16:16).

II. Identifying the Church

Christ's great purpose in history was to build his church (Matt. 16:18). We would be naive not to address the fact that Satan has his own preachers, his own doctrines and his own churches (2 Cor. 11:3, 13-15). Fortunately, the nature of Christ's church (her essential being) is of a quality that manifests a distinct identity. This identity enables Christ's church to be distinguished from counterfeits. The following defines the church's essential nature and identity.

A. The Body of Christ

Paul speaks of the church as the spiritual body of Christ on earth over which Jesus is head (Eph. 1:22-23; Col. 1:18).

B. The Saved Body of Christ

Whom the Lord saves he adds to his church (Acts 2:47). Salvation and membership in the church of Christ are simultaneous. When we elect to receive the saving grace of God by an obedience of faith in Christ, the Lord adds us to the body of the saved. It is not a denomination to be joined by human choice. The church constitutes the universal body of the saved from sin. As a natural consequence of receiving salvation, one necessarily becomes a part of that body of saved people. We thus identify the church by identifying the body of the saved.

C. Those Purchased by the Blood of Christ

Christians are former slaves to sin who have been redeemed from the auction block. The redemptive price was Christ's blood (Eph. 1:7; 1 Peter 1:18-19). The church was purchased by the blood of Christ (Acts 20:28). The church is therefore composed of all who have been redeemed by Christ's blood. If we can identify those who have been blood purchased, we can identify the church.

D. The Sanctified

Paul writes to "the church of God which is at Corinth, to those who are sanctified in Christ Jesus, called to be saints" (1 Cor. 1:1-2). The church is the body of the sanctified, the set apart from sin. The church is to be identified by identifying the sanctified.

E.   The Body of the Reconciled

God reconciles sinners to himself through Christ (2 Cor. 5:18-19). But when we are reconciled, it is "in one body" (Eph. 2:16). The church is the body of the reconciled. We identify the church the same way we identify the body of the reconciled.

F.   The Cleansed, the Washed in Water by the Word

"Husbands, love your wives, just as Christ loved the church and gave himself for it, that he might sanctify and cleanse it with the washing of water by the word" (Eph. 5:25-26). The church is composed of those who have been cleansed when washed (or loosed) from sins by Christ's blood (Rev. 1:5). But the church is cleansed when washed with water by the word. The word "washed" in Ephesians 5:26 is *loutro*, literally "washing." From *louo,* it means to bathe the whole body. This is distinct from *nipto* which means to wash a part of the body, as when Jesus washed the disciples' feet (John 13:1-5). The only water in Christianity for washing the whole body is the water of baptism as commanded in the Word of God (Matt. 28:19; Acts 2:38; 10:48). It is conclusive that we are washed with the blood of Christ when we are washed with water by the word. Those so washed constitute the church. To identify the church we need only to identify how sinful men are washed and cleansed from sin.

G.   Those Who Are in Christ

Paul wrote, "To the church of the Thessalonians in God the Father and the Lord Jesus Christ" (1 Thess. 1:1; 2 Thess. 1:1). All who are "in Christ" constitute the church. We can identify the church when we learn how sinners get into Christ.

H.   Those Who Are Registered in Heaven

The Bible speaks of Christians whose names are in the book of life (Phil. 4:3; Rev. 20:15). But Hebrews speaks of the "church of the firstborn who are registered in heaven" (Heb.

12:23).[9] The church is composed of all whose names are in the book of life.

In summary, the church is the body of all the saved, the redeemed, the reconciled to God, the sanctified. Can one be saved outside the church? We might as well ask if one can be saved without being saved or reconciled? The church of Christ is the universal body of the saved.

The inherent nature of the church is significant to its identity. Inasmuch as the church is the body of the saved, we have but to identify how men are saved, and the church will immediately manifest her identity.

III. How Men Are Saved and Enter the Church

As morally free and responsible human beings we are not compelled to accept God's saving grace by any divine predeterminism. Having been created in the image of God with the power of free choice, we are responsible for our actions. On this ground God will bring all men into account at judgment (2 Cor. 5:10). To be saved, men must learn the gospel and God's required response. False teachings have been widely substituted for the truth of God's requirement. We must stress that our response must agree with what the Lord requires in his Word.

A. The Law of Pardon and Induction into the Church

We must assume that whatever Scripture requires for the salvation of alien sinners is God's immutable and universal law of pardon. When that law is obeyed, God subsequently adds the saved to the church. Thus, there is a divine law of pardon and induction into the church. We have only to identify God's law of pardon, and we shall identify both the means of entrance into the church and those who constitute the church.

B. The Law of Pardon: Obedience to a Pattern of Teaching

Paul reminds the Roman church how and when they were saved:

But God be thanked that though you were slaves of
sin, yet you obeyed from the heart that form of doctrine to which you were delivered. And having been
set free from sin, you became slaves of righteousness (Rom. 6:17-18).

Scripture says that they sincerely obeyed a certain form
of teaching in order to be saved. The word "form" is *tupon*
(from *tupos*) translated as "standard" in the Revised Standard
Version and as "pattern" in the New English Bible. These
Christians were saved (set free from sin) when they obeyed a
certain pattern of teaching (doctrine) that they were taught (delivered). That pattern of teaching is the divine law of pardon.
That pattern of teaching and their obedience to it are record-
ed earlier in the chapter:

How shall we who died to sin live any longer in it?
Or do you not know that as many of us as were baptized into Christ Jesus were baptized into his death?
Therefore we were buried with him through baptism into death, that just as Christ was raised from
the dead by the glory of the Father, even so we also
should walk in newness of life (Rom. 6:2-4).

Paul retraces the very moment when the Romans "died
to sin" and were raised to new life in Christ: when they obeyed
a specified pattern of teaching, God's law of pardon. Paul defines both *what* they did to die to sin and *when* they died to
sin: when they were baptized into Christ and into his death.
The pattern of teaching, the law of pardon, that makes men
free from sin includes baptism into Christ.

C. Induction into the Church

When sinners are saved by sincere obedience to the pattern of teaching, the Lord immediately adds them to the church
(Acts 2:47; 1 Cor. 12:13; cf. Eph. 2:16).

Here, then, is the law of pardon and induction into the
church. By the law of pardon, we identify both the means of
entry into the church and those who constitute the church.

IV. The Relation of Baptism to the Law of Pardon[10]

Christ commissioned the apostles to make disciples of all men by teaching faith, repentance and baptism for remission of sins (Matt. 28:19; Mark 16:15-16; Luke 24:44-47). The rest of the New Testament records the apostles' evangelism and the baptismal response of sinners for salvation. The book of Acts is especially clear in this regard (see diagram of conversions in Acts). Baptism is mentioned in all 10 cases. Acts records in summary that everyone heard the same thing, believed the same thing and did the same thing to get the same thing: salvation from sin and membership in the church. There emerges from this an obvious pattern of obedience for salvation in which baptism is an essential part.

A. The Design of Baptism

1. There is but one baptism. The New Testament teaches there is "one baptism" (Eph. 4:5). Yet we read of the baptism of John and the baptism of the Holy Spirit. However, John's baptism passed away with the Old Covenant (Act 18:24-19:5). The baptism of the Holy Spirit, administered by Christ (Matt. 3:11), was a promise to be received, not a command to be obeyed. It was accomplished at Pentecost (Acts 2:1-21, 33). The "one baptism" under the New Covenant is the baptism of the Great Commission (Matt. 28:18-20). The idea of "one baptism" distinguishes it from the design and purposes of other baptisms. This is true of John's baptism which was superseded by Christ's and of other baptisms that would later pervert either the design or purpose of the "one baptism."

2. Baptism is immersion. Baptism is not merely *by* immersion; it *is* immersion. From *bapto*, to dip, comes *baptizo*, meaning to immerse, plunge, dip, submerge. In the case of Holy Spirit baptism, the word means "overwhelm." *Baptizo* cannot be translated by the words "sprinkle" or "pour." The words "sprinkle" and "pour" come from different Greek words: *rhantizo*, sprinkle, and *cheo*, pour. The words "sprinkle" and "pour" can no more be substituted for the word baptism than can *rhantizo* be substituted for *baptizo*. *Baptizma* means immersion, submersion. This is how the word should be translated in our Bibles (e.g., "one Lord, one faith, one immersion," Eph. 4:5). What Christ and the apostles commanded is immersion.

The word "baptism" is not a proper translation of the word *baptisma* (as in Eph. 4:5). It is more of a transliteration, bringing the sound of the word over into the vernacular. Today the word "baptism" actually conveys no universally accepted specific action outside of a particular church tradition. Thus "baptism" means one thing to one church tradition (e.g., immersion), and another thing to a different church tradition (e.g., sprinkling or pouring). The definition and correct translation of the original word seem to have been tossed aside to accommodate substitutes for immersion which were added centuries after the New Testament was written. [11]

3. Baptism is a burial in water (Rom. 6:4; Col. 2:12). The analogy of baptism to a "burial" corresponds to both the dying of the sinner to his sins in a watery grave and to the fact that baptism, which is immersion, is indeed a burial in water. Thus the New Testament says of the baptism of the Ethiopian eunuch, "Both Philip and the eunuch went down into the water, and he baptized him." Then it says, "They came up out of the water" (Acts 8:38-39). To be a "burial," as Scripture says, requires immersion, a going down into water and a coming up out of water.

B.   The Purpose of Baptism

For those who would follow Christ, baptism is not an option. It is a command. The purpose of baptism is stated in the following:

1. To become the Lord's possession. "Go therefore and make disciples of all the nations, baptizing them *in the name of* the Father and of the Son and of the Holy Spirit" (Matt. 28:19). The phrase, *eis to onoma*, "in the name of," or more correctly, "*into* the name of," does not mean that we are to be baptized "at the command of" or "on the authority of"[12] (as in Acts 2:38 where the phrase is different, *epi to onomati*). "In the Greek *papyri* 'into the name' was a 'common phrase for transference of ownership.' "[13] It was understood to mean, "into the possession of." William Hendriksen writes, "Being baptized into the name of, therefore means being baptized into vital relationship with that One."[14]

W. E. Vine says, "The phrase in Matt. 28:19, 'baptizing them into the Name' ... would indicate that the baptized person was closely bound to, or became the property of, the one into whose Name he was baptized."[15] Myron S. Augsburger adds, "Matthew says we are to baptize '*into the name of ...*' bringing persons into direct relation with God as we know Him: Creator, Redeemer, and Sanctifier."[16]

In each New Testament usage with baptism, *eis to onoma* means that sinners were baptized into the possession of the Lord (see Acts 8:16; 19:5; 1 Cor. 1:13). This is not a formula of words required to be spoken over the one baptized. Rather it speaks of what happens to those who are baptized into the name of the Father, Son, and Holy Spirit. They are baptized *into the possession* of the Father, Son, and Holy Spirit. J. D. Bales explains:

> The word "in" in the King James Version is the same word that is translated "into" in the American Standard Version. The Greek word is *eis* and means into, in, toward, to, in order to... To be baptized into the name of the Father, and of the Son, and of the Holy Spirit indicated that one was baptized into their possession. Thus the one who is baptized belongs to them. [17]

To be baptized into the name of the Father, Son and Holy Spirit in Matthew 28:19 is no different from being baptized into the name of the Lord Jesus in Acts 19:5. The phrases and the meaning are the same in both passages. In Paul's effort to correct the division in the Corinthian church and their fallacy in calling themselves after Paul or Apollos or Cephas, he asked, "Were you baptized in the name of Paul?" (1 Cor. 1:13). The phrase again is *eis to onoma*. He knew their answer to his rhetorical question would be an emphatic, "No." They were baptized into the name of Christ, not Paul; therefore, they were Christ's possession, not Paul's possession. Thus they should call themselves after Christ and not after Paul or other men.

Commenting on 1 Corinthians 1:13 and its meaning Neil Lightfoot observes, "Paul is saying that they do not belong to him because they were not baptized *eis to onoma Paulou.* Moulton and Milligan say that *eis to onoma* frequently occurs in the papyri in reference to payments made 'to the account of' someone. Upon this basis they further remark: 'The usage is of interest in connection with Matt. 28:19, where the meaning would seem to be "baptized into the possession of the Father."' This is one illustration of multitudes which demonstrates the vital importance of the papyri in shedding light on the message of the N.T."[18]

Evangelicals like David Prior and F.W. Grosheide agree in their comments on 1 Corinthians 1:13. Prior writes:

> To be baptized in (*eis*, literally "into") the name of someone was to have one's life signed over to that person, to come under his authority and to be at his beck and call. Paul makes the self-evident point that the Corinthians had, in baptism, become the possession of Jesus Christ – and of nobody else. [19]

Grosheide adds, "To be baptized into the name of someone means to be brought into the most intimate relation with this person's revelation" (cf Matt. 28:19). [20]

William Barclay has written, "The phrase *into the name of* implied absolute and utter possession."[21] James. D. Bales has observed, "Baptism into the name indicates that one belongs to the one into whose name he is baptized. In baptism we are baptized into the name of the Father, the Son, and the Holy Spirit. We enter into their possession."[22]

Paul said that Jesus died to "purify for himself his own special people" (Titus 2:14), or "a people for his own possession" (as in the ASV and NASB). Jesus died to make us his possession, and he does so when we are baptized into his name.

One of the purposes of baptism is to make us the possession of the Lord. [23]

2. Jesus requires faith and baptism for salvation. "And he said to them, 'Go into all the world and preach the gospel to every creature. He who believes and is baptized will be saved; but he who does not believe will be condemned' " (Mark 16:15-16).

Who is the "he" that will be saved? He who believes *and* is baptized. We observe this teaching reproduced in the conversion of the Samaritans (Acts 8:12), Simon the sorcerer (Acts 8:13), the eunuch (Acts 8:26-39), the Philippian jailer (Acts 16:30-34), the Corinthians (Acts 18:8), and the Galatians (Gal. 3:26-27).

3. Peter requires baptism for salvation and a clear conscience. On Pentecost following Christ's resurrection, God gave birth to his church by saving three thousand souls who responded with faith, repentance and baptism as commanded by the apostle Peter (Acts 2:37-41). When asked what to do by the multitude who had been convinced by the apostles' preaching that Jesus was Lord and Christ, Peter replied, "Repent, and be baptized everyone of you in the name of Jesus Christ for the remission of sins, and you shall receive the gift of the Holy Spirit." On that day the church of Christ began with three thousand souls who "gladly received his word" in baptism.

Luke further explains that all who were saved thereafter were added to the same church (2:47). Faith is clearly connected to repentance and baptism for forgiveness of sins and to receiving the gift of the Holy Spirit.

Peter teaches that baptism now saves us (1 Peter 3:21) and explains that the guilty conscience of the alien sinner is cleansed when he responds to God in baptism as "an appeal to God for a good conscience" (1 Peter 3:21 NASB). The translation of the RSV is equally clear, stating that baptism is "an appeal to God for a clear conscience." This agrees with the book of Hebrews that the conscience is cleansed when we "draw near with a true heart in full assurance of faith having our hearts sprinkled from an evil conscience and our bodies washed with pure water" (Heb. 9:14; 10: 22).

When the alien sinner, whose guilt has been brought to bear upon his conscience through hearing the gospel, responds to Christ in baptism, it is for salvation and consequent cleansing of his guilty conscience. The New Testament teaches that sinners with guilty consciences are to be baptized, not sinners with clear consciences.

Consider also that Jesus shed his blood "for the remission of sins" (Matt. 26:28), but Peter commands repentance and baptism "for the remission of sin" (Acts 2:38). Therefore we receive the redemptive benefit of the blood of Christ when we are baptized.

4. Paul explains the purpose(s) of baptism:

a. To wash away sins. Luke records Paul's own account of his conversion and the stated reason for his baptism (Acts 22:1-16). He says the Lord sent Ananias to baptize him, who stated, "And now why are you waiting? Arise and be baptized, and wash away your sins, calling on the name of the Lord." The purpose of baptism in this account is clear; it is to wash away sins.

This account is a good commentary on what Peter meant at Pentecost when he said, "And it shall come to pass that whoever calls on the name of the Lord shall be saved" (Acts 2:21). To call on the name of the Lord obviously did not mean to pray for salvation inasmuch as Peter commanded repentance and baptism for salvation (2:38). To call on the Lord's name for salvation meant to respond to his authority by obeying his command.

On Pentecost three thousand called on Christ's name for salvation by receiving his word to repent and be baptized for remission of sins. The meaning of Ananias' words to Paul was the same. He was to arise to be baptized to wash away his sins, and by that means he called on the authoritative name of the Lord for salvation as did the Jews on Pentecost.

b. To become the possession of Christ. As observed above, Paul taught, as did Jesus in the great commission (Matt. 8:19), that sinners are to be baptized to become the possession of Christ (Acts 19:1-5; 1 Cor. 1:13).

c. To die to sin, to be raised to a new life with Christ, to unite with Christ, to be freed or justified from sin (Rom. 6:1-7). In Romans 6:17-18 Paul reminds the church of what they were (bondslaves to sin), of what they did (obeyed a pattern of teaching), and of what they became (free from sin). This obedience is described in 6:1-7 when they were baptized to die to sin (2-4), to be raised to walk in newness of life (4), to be united with Christ (5), to do away with the body of sin (6) and to be freed from sin, or justified (7).[24] The pattern of teaching to be obeyed by all sinners in order to die to sin essentially embraces baptism.

d. To enter the body of Christ, the church (1 Cor. 12:13). The Holy Spirit baptizes us into the body of the church the same way he enables all men to confess that Jesus is Lord, that is, by the word of his instruction (1 Cor. 12:3).

e. For the redemption of the body at the resurrection (1 Cor. 15:29). The saved already have eternal life (1 John 5:1-4; 11-13). We are waiting now for the redemption of our bodies which will die and decay (Romans 8:18-23). At the resurrection our bodies will be reconstituted, raised and glorified (Phil. 3:20-21; 1 Cor. 15:12-49).

First century Christians seemed to have been fairly well instructed on the redemption of our bodies at the resurrection which is sealed at our baptism. As Paul said, "Otherwise, what will they do that are baptized for the dead, if the dead do not rise at all? Why then are they baptized for the dead?" (1 Cor. 15:29). We are baptized to receive eternal life and the redemption of our bodies.

f. To put on Christ, to be clothed with Christ. The Roman boy becomes a man and puts on his toga, and the Jew leaves his minor status and dons the clothing of his adult manhood (Gal. 3:26-27). In this analogy is the idea of the heir who reaches the age of his inheritance. The sons of Abraham were to inherit justification by faith as promised in Genesis 12:3 (Gal. 3:6-9). Paul teaches it is by faith in Christ expressed in baptism that we become sons and consequently heirs of the promise of justification.

g. To be sanctified, cleansed (Eph. 5:25-26). Paul reminds the church that Christ sanctified and cleansed it "with the washing of water by the word." In the New Testament the only washing in water (bathing the whole body) for cleansing according to the Lord's word is baptism.

h. To put off the body of sins (Col. 2:11-12). When God saves men from sin, he cuts away, puts off, their sins. The language reveals a clear analogy to circumcision used to express the action of God in cutting away or "putting off" the body of sins. Paul does not say baptism is circumcision or a type of circumcision. He plainly defines this circumcision as "putting off the body of the sins of the flesh" (11). But *when* does God spiritually circumcise men? God spiritually circumcises the sinner when he is baptized for remission of sins. Baptism, says Paul, is the expression of our faith in God to raise us from the dead in sin even as he raised Christ from the dead (12).

5. Baptism is only for those who:

a. Can be taught to be disciples of Christ, (Matt. 28:19). Christ's command is to baptize those who have been taught.

b. Can believe the gospel (Mark 16:15-16).

c. Can repent of their sins (Acts 2:38).

d. Can arise of their own free will and be baptized (Acts 22:16).

e. Can obey from the heart the form of teaching to make one free from sin (Rom. 6:17-18; 6:1-7).

f. Can have guilty consciences because of their sins (1 Peter 3:21).

It is interesting to note that none of the above can apply to babies.

In summary, New Testament baptism is defined in both its design and purpose. It has a distinct identity. Any baptism (immersion) by a different design or for a different purpose is not the "one baptism" defined, commanded and practiced in Scripture.

V. The Non-Denominational Nature of the Church

A. Definition of a Denomination

Protestant denominationalism is new to Christianity; it did not exist until the 16th century. The term "denomination" is neither a Bible word nor a Bible subject.[25] A definition of a denomination is therefore dependent upon the history and doctrine of denominationalism. This considered, a denomination can be defined as *a doctrinally distinct body of professed Christians, but not the only Christians, who believe that they have been saved by grace through faith in Christ apart from any other requirement and who have denominated themselves with a distinctive name by which they distinguish their characteristic doctrine and practice from other denominations.*

B. Distinguishing the New Testament Church from Denominations

The major distinction between modern evangelical denominations and the church in the New Testament is the doctrine of the salvation of alien sinners. [26] Evangelical denominations characteristically teach that salvation is by faith alone and that baptism therefore constitutes no part of the kind of faith by which alien sinners are justified. This leads to the further denial that baptism is an essential prerequisite to forgiveness of sins.

However, this doctrine stands in contrast to the New Testament teaching that (1) men are *not* justified by faith alone (James 2:14-26), (2) that alien sinners are saved by an *obedience* of faith in Christ (Rom. 1:5; 16:25-26), (3) that saving faith is *perfected* by works of faith (James 2: 21-23), (4) and that baptism *is* for the forgiveness of sins (Acts 2:38).

C. The Church of Christ Is Not a Denomination

The divine doctrine of salvation is of utmost significance to distinguish the church from a denomination. A denomination, as defined above, does not identify with the New

Testament church as the body of the saved by faith, repentance and baptism.

VI. Conclusion

Since the church is the body of all the saved in Christ, it can be identified by the doctrinal means required for man's salvation.

Quick-Answer Questions

1. What is the church?
2. Can one be saved outside the church? Why or why not?
3. Is there a law of pardon for all to obey for salvation?
4. What is the relation of baptism to salvation?
5. What is the relation of baptism to the church?
6. Does one have to be in the church to be saved? Why?

Discussion Questions

1. Explain how the Lord's church can be identified.
2. What does "into the name of" mean in Matthew 28:19? Explain the purpose of baptism according to Matthew 28:19. Elaborate on Paul's purpose for asking the Corinthians if they had been "baptized into the name of Paul" (1 Cor. 1:13).
3. What does "in the name of" mean in Acts 2:38? Elaborate on Peter's meaning to be "baptized in the name of Jesus Christ."
4. Explain how men enter the church.
5. Explain why we are not to baptize people whose consciences are clear.
6. Explain the difference between the church of Christ and a denomination.

CHAPTER 4

THE ESTABLISHMENT OF THE CHURCH

After Peter confessed that Jesus was the Christ, the son of the living God, Jesus announced his purpose to build his church (Matt. 16:13-18). At that time the church was yet future — "*will* build." Later Luke tells us that "great fear came upon all the church" (Acts 5:11). Obviously at this time the church was in existence.[27] Therefore sometime between Christ's pledge to build the church and Luke's statement that it was in existence, the church was established.

At the same time, following Peter's confession, Jesus pledged the keys to throw open the kingdom (Matt. 16:19). That, too, was yet future – "*will* give you the keys." At that time the doors of Christ's reign were not yet opened for citizenship. Later Paul speaks of the kingdom as being in place and the saints being translated into it (Col. 1:12-13). Correspondingly, between the time Jesus said he would bestow the keys of the kingdom and Paul's statement that saints were being translated into it, the kingdom came.

The purpose of this lesson is to see the interrelationship of the church to the kingdom of God and to trace the establishment of the church in regard to time, power and place.

I. The Church and the Kingdom Are Interrelated

Lexicographers define "kingdom" with a primary meaning of royal power, kingship, rule and reign. The secondary meaning embraces territory and realm. The primary meaning of sovereign rule allows comprehension of a number of Scriptures where the idea of realm would either confuse or inadequately convey the sovereign reign of Christ back of his realm (e.g. Dan. 7:14a,[28] 27; Matt. 5:3,10; 16:28,[29] John 3:3; Luke 17:20-21; Rom. 14:17). In other Scriptures realm seems to be the idea (e.g. Dan. 4:25; Matt. 4:8; 19:23; John 3:5; Rev. 5:9-10).

While the term "church" is not always co-extensive with the term "kingdom," the terms have nonetheless been interrelated since the church was established. Christ promised, "I will build my church… I will give you the keys of the kingdom" (Matt. 16:18-19). Seeing the interrelationship of the church and the kingdom will enable one to understand that with the establishment of the church came the full realization of the kingdom of Old Testament prophecy, the reign of God through his Christ. In the church the Jew finds all of the kingdom prophecies to Israel fulfilled. It is the church for which Christ exercises his sovereign reign (Eph. 1:19-22). It is the church that receives the kingdom (Heb. 12:28). The church is Christ's kingdom of willing subjects on earth. The church manifests the sovereignty of Christ in the hearts and lives of men by their obedience of faith. The kingdom is not to be viewed as a future development; it is a present reality. With the coming of the church, Christ assumed his sovereign reign.

A. Jesus Interrelated the Terms Church and Kingdom (Matt. 16:18-19)

Perhaps we should see the terms "church" and "kingdom" as interrelated in this Scripture rather than interchangeable.

B. Both Church and Kingdom Are Composed of Saints

Paul writes to "the church of God which is at Corinth, to those who are sanctified in Christ Jesus, called to be saints" (1 Cor. 1:2). The church is composed of "saints." To the Colossians he says that God "has qualified us to be partakers of the inheritance of the saints in light. He has delivered us from the power of darkness and translated us into the kingdom of the son of his love" (Col. 1:12-13). The saints are translated into the kingdom. Since both the church and the kingdom are composed of the saints, they have to be interrelated.

C. Both Church and Kingdom Are Composed of Blood-purchased Men

Acts 20:28 speaks of "the church of God which he purchased with his own blood." John said of Christ, "You were slain, and have redeemed us to God by your blood out of every tribe and tongue and people and nation, and have made us kings and priests to our God; and we shall reign on the earth" (Rev. 5:9-10). Other versions translate "kings" with the word "kingdom." The kingdom is also purchased, redeemed, by Christ's blood. Consequently, the people that comprise the kingdom are equated with the people that comprise the church.

D. Priests of the House Are Priests in the Kingdom

The church is God's spiritual house (1 Tim. 3:15), and God's spiritual house is made of holy priests (1 Peter 2:5). The kingdom is comprised of those priests (Rev. 5:9-10). Therefore, the church, God's house, is comprised of the priests that comprise the kingdom. The kingdom and the church are so interrelated they cannot be separated.

II. The Time for the Establishment of the Kingdom

The gospels tell us how close the kingdom was during the ministries of John the Baptist and Jesus.

A. The Kingdom of God Was "At Hand"

This is the message of John the Baptist (Matt. 3:1-2), the message of Jesus (Matt. 4:17; Mark 1:15), the message Jesus commanded the 12 apostles (Matt. 10:1,7), and the message Jesus commanded the 70 to preach (Luke 10:1,9). When a thing is "at hand," it is near. If the kingdom of God is not now here, it was not *near* when they said it was.

B. Some of that Generation Would Be Alive When the Kingdom Came (Mark 9:1)

If the kingdom has not yet come, there are some men of Christ's generation who are yet alive today! In point of time the kingdom was to come during the generation in which the Lord lived on earth.

III. The Power and Place of the Kingdom's Establishment

Both the power of the Holy Spirit required to inaugurate the kingdom and the city of Jerusalem (where the kingdom was to begin) are detailed.

A. The Power: The Holy Spirit

Jesus foretold that some in his presence would not "taste death" before they would "see the kingdom of God present with *power*" (Mark 9:1). He later said to his apostles that they would be "endued with *power* from on high" (Luke 24:49) and stated that they would receive that power with the coming of the Holy Spirit (Acts 1:8).

B. The Place: The City of Jerusalem

Before his ascension, Christ instructed the apostles to "tarry in the city of Jerusalem until you are endued with power from on high" (Luke 24:49). The place to which the Holy Spirit would come with power was the city of Jerusalem.

Thus the kingdom would come with power, the power would come with the Holy Spirit and the Holy Spirit would bestow the power upon the apostles in the city of Jerusalem. When the Spirit came upon the apostles, the kingdom came.

IV. The Day and Time of the Establishment of the Church / Kingdom

With the establishment of the church, the Davidic prophecies are fulfilled. In Acts 2:22-36 Peter argues for the resurrection and exaltation of Jesus on the right hand of God and therefore to the promised throne of David. He announces the coronation and sovereign reign of Jesus Christ. He explains that the prophecy of 2 Samuel 7:11-16 promised to David that his seed would sit and reign over his kingdom forever, and the prophecies in Psalm 16:9-11 and Psalm 110:1, that were prophesied by David regarding the resurrection of Christ, were fulfilled in the resurrection of Jesus and his consequent exaltation to the throne of David. Peter implies that by the resurrection Jesus was "therefore exalted to the right hand of God" to sit on David's throne. He reasons that with the resurrection and exaltation of Jesus to the throne of David the kingdom prophecies are fulfilled. Peter then concludes that all the house of Israel should know by this that God made Jesus both Lord and Christ.

A.   The Day of Pentecost (Acts 2:1-4)

Pentecost was the old Jewish festival of first fruits that took place at the beginning of the wheat harvest. It occurred annually fifty days after Passover (Lev. 23:4-16). In this case Pentecost came fifty days after the Lord's death and resurrection.

B.   The Third Hour of the Day, 9 a.m. (Acts 2:15)

Peter is speaking to the Jewish audience using Jewish terminology. Since the Jews distinguished their daytime hours – about 6 a.m. to 6 p.m. – from their night time hours – about 6 p.m. to 6 a.m. – (John 11:9-10), "the third hour of the day" would correspond to 9 a.m. our time.

C.   The Establishment of the Church / Kingdom

When on Pentecost the Holy Spirit was poured out on the apostles, they preached Christ crucified and raised. Three thousand Israelites were convinced Jesus was Lord and Christ and were baptized (Acts 2:1-41). These were "added to the church" (Acts 2:47). Thus, we know the time and place of the establishment of the church and the power with which it came. But the kingdom would come when the power came. Thus, with the establishment of the church came the kingdom reign of Christ for the redemption of ruined humanity. [30]

V.   Conclusion

Before Pentecost the church and the kingdom are referred to as future. From Pentecost onward they are referred to as present realities. Fifty days after the resurrection, the reign of Christ Jesus was announced, and the church was established in the city of Jerusalem. Once again we observe marks of identity of the church: the time, the place, the power and the day of establishment.

Identity is the thing sought, not succession. We are not concerned with tracing a line of succession from the apostles to today but of identifying the church revealed in the New Testament.

Quick-Answer Questions

1.   Are the terms "church" and "kingdom" always co-extensive?
2.   Of what are both church and kingdom composed?
3.   John, Jesus, the twelve and the seventy preached the kingdom was "at hand." How close was "at hand?" Will Mark 9:1 help?
4.   When did Christ take the rule of the kingdom of God? What Scripture(s) so teach?
5.   When and where was the church established?
6.   According to Acts 2:41, 47 to *what* church are the saved added today?

Discussion Questions

1.   Discuss some implications of believing the kingdom is yet future.
2.   In light of the primary definition of the term "kingdom," expand on the meaning of Matthew 5:3; 6:31-33; Luke 17:20-21 and Romans 14:17.
3.   Christ began his reign on the day the church was established (Acts 2:22-47). Elaborate on the interrelationship of the kingdom and the church.
4.   Explain how it is that when the saved are added to the

church (Acts 2:47), the saints at the same time are translated into the kingdom (Col. 1:12-13).

PART TWO

THE ORGANIZATIONAL STRUCTURE OF THE CHURCH

"That things were to be done orderly and systematically, even as Paul commanded the Corinthians (1 Cor. 14:40) and for which he commended the Colossians (Col. 2:5), was carried out throughout the organizational structure of the local church... The example of these early New Testament churches becomes the pattern for local churches today. As a representation of the church universal, the body of Christ, each local church should have the symmetry, the beauty, the decorum, the orderliness characteristic of the archetype" (Earl C. Radmacher, *What the Church Is All About*, 354, 355).

"Right up to the year 100 (if you take the book of Revelation as having been written then) John, writing under the inspiration of the Holy Spirit, directs the book of Revelation to individual churches. Hence, up to the end of the New Testament, individual churches existed and were important enough for letters to be addressed to them. The picture is clear: As Paul moves over the Roman Empire, as Aquila and Priscilla move over the Roman Empire, as other Christians move over the Roman Empire, individuals are saved and local churches are organized. And this, I believe, is a pattern that holds for the church till Jesus comes" (Francis Schaeffer, *The Church At the End of the 20th Century,* 62.).

CHAPTER 5

CHRIST THE HEAD AND FOUNDATION OF THE CHURCH

The structural form of the church revealed in the New Testament stands in marked contrast to those organizational innovations which have been attached to the church since apostolic times. The structural design of the apostolic church is sufficient to govern the church in her mission and worship and to provide for the physical needs, the spiritual development and the emotional stability of her members.

This lesson presents Christ as the divine head of the church and as such the very foundation rock upon which the church is built.

I. Christ: The Head of the Church

When we raise the question of the governance of the church, we ask who has the *right* to speak. The Bible claims that right for Christ alone.

A. Christ Has All Authority (Matt. 28:18-20)

Christ's authority is sovereign and universal, extending to all realms "in heaven and on earth" (cf. 1 Peter 3:22). His command to "Go *therefore* and make disciples of all nations ... teaching them to observe all things that *I* have commanded" comes out of his claim to have all authority. Inherent in authority is the right to govern, to command, to lead and, consequently, to speak.

1. Christ's word: the standard of final judgment (John 12:48; cf Acts 17:31). The question of authority is of prime importance. Most religious differences would be resolved by an appeal to Christ's authoritative word.

2. The apostles' word: the authority of Christ. The apostles were specially chosen to represent Christ and ultimately the Father himself (John 13:20). Jesus promised the Holy Spirit to the apostles for special guidance into "all truth" (John 14:26; 16:13). At Pentecost the Holy Spirit came to the apostles (Acts 2:1-4; 4:8). From that time they spoke by the guidance of the Spirit (1 Cor. 2:4, 6-13; 11:23; 2 Cor. 4:5-6; 5:18-20; 1 Thess. 4:8, 15; 5:27; 1 Tim. 4:1; 1 Peter 1:12). Their word is the Word of God.

B.   Christ: The Head of the Church (Eph. 5:23; Col. 1:18)

The church has received the command to honor the authority of Christ: "And whatever you do in word or deed, do all in the name of the Lord Jesus" (Col. 3:17). What we do "in the name of" Christ we do by the authority of the word of Christ (as in Acts 2:38; 10:48; 1 Cor. 6:11).

Men often attribute differences in faith and practice to difficulties of interpretation. However, most religious differences have their origin in the acceptance of a different authority than the authority of Christ's word.

C.   Christ: Lawgiver and Judge (James 4:12)

These two seats are reserved for Christ: "There is one lawgiver, who is able to save and to destroy. Who are you to judge another?" In Christ alone reside the powers of legislation (given in the New Covenant) and judgment (both historically and finally).

In summary, Christ Jesus stands absolute in his authority at the head of his church. No one other than those especially appointed by Christ in the first century can claim to speak for Christ and still respect the authority of Christ in the New Testament.

II. Christ: The Foundation of the Church

Jesus said, "On this rock I would build my church, and the gates of Hades shall not prevail against it" (Matt. 16:18). The church stands upon the work that Christ accomplished at the cross and proved in his resurrection. He is the church's one foundation. The doctrine of Christ as the foundation of the church is not mere theology unrelated to the Christian's life. It is the real motive of the Christian's faith and service. If Christ was raised from the dead, he can raise us. If he was not raised, his death was but a meaningless sentiment. Upon belief in the historical resurrection of Christ, the church has founded her confidence for an eternal future with God.

In this part of the lesson, we will discuss what that "rock" is, why Hades will not prevail against the church and the place of the apostles in the church's foundation.

A. The Foundation in Prophecy

1. "A tried stone" (Isa. 28:16). Isaiah foretold that the foundation stone for God's house would be tried and proven.

2. A "rejected" stone (Ps. 118:22). The stone selected by God would be rejected by "the builders," that is, the Jews.

B. Peter's Confession and Christ's Claims (Matt. 16:13-18)

When Christ asked his disciples to tell what others were thinking of him, they replied, "Some say John the Baptist, some Elijah, and others Jeremiah or one of the prophets." When the apostles were asked what they believed, Peter replied, "You are the Christ, the son of the living God."

1. Peter confesses Jesus' deity. What Peter confessed was the divine nature of Jesus, his deity. Since like begets like and God is divine, then Jesus, as the son of God, is divine. Jesus' divine nature, his Godhood, is the foundation rock upon which the church is built. The church is built upon neither Peter nor his confession, but upon the thing confessed: the divine sonship of Jesus. Faith in Jesus as the son of God who is able to save us from sin, raise us from the dead and give us eternal life will lead us to build our eternal hope on him. Jesus, then, as the divine son of God, is the foundation rock upon which the church is built.

2. Jesus claims death shall not prevail against the church. Hades is the place of disembodied spirits. Hades is not hell (*gehenna*), the final place of the condemned, but the intermediate state of the dead. All who die go to the hadean world to await the final outcome of history. [31] But Hades will not prevail against the church; it will not hold back the church from rising from the dead, for as Christ was raised, he will raise his church.[32]

III. Messianic Prophecies Fulfilled in the Death and Resurrection of Jesus

It was prophesied that the Messiah would be rejected, crucified, buried and resurrected on the third day (cf. 1 Cor. 15:3-4). Inasmuch as Jesus fulfilled these prophecies it is conclusive that He is the Messiah.

A. Jesus Rejected and Crucified by the Jews

The Jews put Jesus to death (Mark 8:31; Acts 2:22-23; 4:10-11), thus fulfilling Psalm 118:22-24.

B. Jesus Raised from the Dead (Matt. 28:1-6; Mark 16:1-6)

At the cross Jesus' claims were tried. In his death and resurrection Jesus was tested and proven to be the son of God, thus fulfilling Isaiah 28:16, "a tried stone...a sure foundation."

C. The Resurrection: Confirmation of Jesus' Deity and Claims (Act 2:22-36; Rom. 1:4)

At Pentecost Peter reasoned from the resurrection to prove that Jesus was both Lord and Christ. On that ground three thousand placed their faith in Jesus and were baptized for the remission of their sins (37-41). Those three thousand constituted the church (47), which was built on faith in Christ as the risen Lord. The church was built on Christ as a house is built on a rock-solid foundation.

Paul appealed to this same reasoning when he said that Jesus was "declared to be the son of God with power, according to the Spirit of holiness, by the resurrection from the dead" (Rom. 1:4). By the resurrection Jesus confirmed his deity, his claim to have power to raise the dead (cf. John 5:28-29; 11:25-26) and his claim that Hades would not prevail against his church. The resurrection is sufficient to sustain men's faith in Christ as God (deity) and to motivate them to build their hope on him for an eternal future.

IV. The Apostles' Declaration that Christ Is the Rock

Christ, in speaking of building His church, uses the analogy of building a house on a foundation of bedrock. In antiquity construction engineers would dig down to bedrock to anchor those massive houses (cf Matt. 7:24-27). The rock upon which Christ would build His house, the church (cf. 1 Tim. 3:15) is His deity. His deity is what Peter confessed when he said that Jesus was the Christ, the Son of the living God (Matt. 16:13-18). This is further explained in the following.

A. Paul's Declaration (1 Cor. 3:11)

"For no other foundation can anyone lay than that which is laid, which is Jesus Christ." It is plain apostolic teaching that Christ is the foundation of the church.

B. Peter's Declaration (1 Peter 2:4-8)

Peter states that Christians have come to Jesus the "living stone," who was rejected by men but made by God to be the foundation stone upon which God's spiritual house is built. Over this truth, like "living stones," Peter says men stumble when they are disobedient to his Word. To the believing and obedient, Christ is "precious" as the "rock" upon which we build for our eternal future.

V. The Place of the Apostles in the Foundation of the Church

Paul said that the "household of God" has "been built upon the foundation of the apostles and prophets" (Eph. 2:18-19). While the authority for Christianity is Christ (Matt. 28:18-20; Eph. 5:23; Col. 1:18; 3:17), all we know of Christ and his commandments is from the writings of his apostles and prophets. The following explains the place of the apostles in the foundation of the church.

A. We Are to Receive the Apostles as We Receive Christ (Luke 10: 16; John 13:20; 20:21-23)

The apostles were sent to forgive and to retain sins. This does not mean that they had the authority to decide whether one should or should not be forgiven and to pronounce him saved or lost. Christ said those who receive the apostles receive Christ and those who receive Christ receive the Father. We receive the apostles by receiving their word (Luke 13:20; Acts 2:41). Only the words of Christ's apostles are sufficient to present the truth of life and death to all men without corruption (cf. 2 Cor. 2:14-17; 3:1-6). When men receive the word of the apostles, they are forgiven by the Lord; when they reject the apostles' word, their sins are retained by the Lord, that is, they will not be forgiven. By this means the apostles forgive and retain sins.

Only the apostles have the authority to speak for Christ (2 Cor. 4:5-6; 5:18-20). Here is the authoritative place of the apostles in the foundation of the church.

B. The Apostles Laid the Church's Foundation (1 Cor. 3:10-11)

The apostles established Christ as the foundation of the church by preaching Christ crucified, buried and raised and by confirming their message by miracles and eyewitness testimony (Mark 16:15-20; Acts 2:22-36; 3:13-15; 5:30-32; 13:30-31; 1 John 1:1-4). The foundation was laid down once for all time to come. We are to build on that one foundation.

C.   The Apostles Bind and Loose (Matt. 16:18-19)

The church is built on the word of Christ as spoken by the apostles, who preach what God has bound. An accurate translation says, "Whatever you shall bind on earth *shall have been bound in heaven*, and whatever you shall loose on earth *shall have been loosed in heaven*" (Matt. 16:19 NASB). Jesus has the apostles binding and loosing only what God has pre-determined to be bound and loosed.[34] Thus at Pentecost the apostles bound faith in Christ and repentance and baptism for remission of sins. Three thousand received their word as the very word of God, sins were loosed and the church began (Acts 2:38-41,47). Thus, the church was built on Jesus as Lord and Christ as declared in the apostles' word.

D.   All Gospel Truth Revealed Through the Apostles

1. Jesus promised the apostles a supernatural endowment of all gospel knowledge (John 14:26; 16:13). Jesus promised the apostles that the Holy Spirit would teach them all things and guide them into all truth.[33] By this means the apostles would know all gospel truth.

2. The New Testament's claim that the apostles received all truth from the Holy Spirit.

a. Luke's claim. The apostles received the Spirit on Pentecost by which they spoke to the people (Acts 2:1-4).

b. Paul's claim. The Holy Spirit imparted to Paul the total revelation of the gospel, which had been a hidden mystery from the foundation of the world (1 Cor. 2:6-13; Eph. 3:3-6).[35] This is tantamount to a claim that Jesus' promise to send the Holy Spirit to teach the apostles "all things" had been fulfilled.

c. Peter's claim. The gospel was preached by men who were guided by the Holy Spirit (1 Peter 1:12). Thus, the Holy Spirit had already come as Jesus promised. Peter also said, "His divine power has given to us all things that pertain to life and godliness, through the knowledge of Him who called us" (2 Peter 1:3). Peter claims the "all things" Jesus promised to the apostles by the Holy Spirit had been fulfilled.

d. John's claim. John prepared the church against the

coming of false teachers. He reminded the brethren that they had already been taught all things (1 John 2:26) and that they knew all things, all gospel truth (1 John 2:20-21). Therefore, he said they needed no other teaching but were to abide in what they had learned (1 John 2:24-27). Obviously the Holy Spirit had already taught all truth to the apostles, who had passed it on to these brethren. The church was cautioned to test everything against the apostles' word by which they would "know the spirit of truth and the spirit of error" (1 John 4:1,6),[36] a claim tantamount to having all truth.

Jesus' claim to send the Holy Spirit to the apostles has been fulfilled. To them was revealed all gospel truth. The apostles then delivered the truth to the church by preaching, and the same truth is resident in their letters. The church is to hold what has been authoritatively delivered whether by word (preaching) or letter (2 Thess. 2:15). Their word is the place of the apostles in the foundation of the church.

E.   The Apostles' Word the Ground of Faith in Christ (John 17:20)

Jesus said the basis of the Christian's faith is the apostles' word. John said he wrote his gospel that men might believe (John 19:35; 20:30-31). Paul taught that faith in Christ "comes by hearing, and hearing by the word of God" (Rom. 10:17). Only the apostles were commissioned and empowered to represent Christ in their word (2 Cor. 2: 14-17; 4:1-6; 5:18-20).

The faith God wants us to have does not come from subjective feelings, existential experiences or by modern visions or dreams, but from the apostles' word.

VI. Conclusion

The church rests upon the proposition that Jesus is the Christ, the Son of God. He is the "rock" upon which the church continues to be built. Here is another point of identity. Christ's church rests upon the authority of Christ as revealed through the apostles' word.

Quick-Answer Questions

1. What is inherent in authority?
2. What is involved in the statement, Christ is the head of the church?
3. Who and what is the "rock" of Matthew 16:18?
4. What Scripture says Jesus is the foundation of the church?
5. What is Hades? Hell?
6. Who goes to Hades, and who goes to Hell?

Discussion Questions

1. Discuss whether there is legislative authority in the church.
2. Discuss the implications of Christ's authority upon such statements as, "My preacher says" and "Our church teaches."
3. Discuss (1) the analogy of Jesus as the foundation rock of the church and (2) how the church is built on Christ.
4. Expand on the practicality of Christ as the rock-solid foundation of the Christian's faithful life.
5. Religious cult leaders often claim to be Christ or representatives of Christ. Explain how founding our lives on Christ according to the apostles' word precludes accepting the claims of cult leaders.
6. Explain what Jesus meant when he said that Hades shall not prevail against the church.
7. Paul said Christ is the only foundation of the church (1 Cor. 3: 10-11). Elaborate on how he could also say the church is built on the foundation of the apostles and prophets (Eph. 2:19).

CHAPTER 6

THE ELDERSHIP

As already observed, the church exists on at least two levels, the universal church and the local congregation. The organizational structure extends to both levels. Since we have examined the structure of the universal church, the next four lessons will deal with the infrastructure the Lord organized for ministry in the local church.

The Lord arranged for the oversight of the local church to be ministered by elders, also called overseers. These are the spiritual shepherds of the local church. This lesson considers their names and their number.

I. Their Names and the Significance of Each

There are three nouns in the Greek New Testament that are descriptive of the character and ministry of elders.

A. Their Names

1. Presbuteros. Translated "presbyter" or "elder," this word refers to an older man, one advanced in life, a senior. Although the word itself carries no official meaning, it shows the dignity of the ministry of elders.

2. Episkopos. Translated "overseer," later to be called "bishop," this word is defined as "a man charged with the duty of seeing that things to be done by others are done rightly, any curator, guardian, or superintendent."[37] In the New Testament the term is used of elders, denoting the watchful care they are to exercise (Acts 20:17-31).[38] A more literal rendering of 1 Timothy 3:1 is "If anyone aspires to oversight he desires a good work." There is no word in this text that can properly be translated "office." The word "overseer" conveys neither the idea of an office nor a title but the job description of the elder, the ministry to be performed.

3. *Poimein.* Properly translated "shepherd" throughout the New Testament, it is translated but once by the word "pastor" (Eph. 4:11).[39] The verb form *poimaino* is analogously used of elders who "*shepherd* the church" as a flock (Acts 20:28).

B. The Age of an Elder

In the Greco-Roman society, in which Paul lived and wrote, the age of an elder was viewed to begin on or about one's 40th year. This is significant for the church today which has seen men in their early to mid-30s rationalize their age into the eldership. The concern here is not merely academic, but practical and scriptural. An elder must possess maturity which only adequate time and experience can provide.

Professor William Barclay addressed the matter saying, "The Apostolic canons later laid it down that a man was not to become a bishop until he was over 50, for by then he will be past youthful disorders."[40] Such an arbitrary age decision was neither apostolic nor wise since it could have kept some good men under 50 from serving as elders. But it does manifest their view of the word "elder." A man in his 30s simply would not have passed the age qualification.

Society in New Testament times saw the 40th year as the termination of a man's youth and entry into an age bracket that would no longer allow him to be conscripted into the military. William M. Ramsay, regarded at the scholastic top of church historians, observed that the word *youth* was a full grown man "… strictly, a full grown man of military age."[41] He also stated, "The word 'youth,' in the strictest Greek usage, begins about twenty and ends with the approach of old age."[42]

Barclay writes, "The word that is used for youth (*neotes*) can in Greek describe anyone of military age, that is, up to the age of 40."[43] This age conception is further documented in *The Interpreter's Bible*: "Youth ... is known to have been applied to full-grown men of military age, up to 40."[44] Paul's "Let no man despise thy youth" (1 Tim. 4:12) has been very generally reckoned by commentators that Timothy was in his mid to late 30s. Hence Vincent notes, "Timothy was probably 38-40 years old at this time."[45] While we might have wondered why Timothy could be called a youth at such an age, historical research has explained the matter.

The age of an elder seems quite clear. No one would have been considered an elder in the church until he was more than 40 years old.

C.   These Terms Designate the Same Ministry-Group

The three Greek words *presbuteros, episkopos, poimein*, from which we translate, elder or presbyter, overseer or bishop, and shepherd or pastor, all refer to the same ministry group of men. This becomes apparent in light of the following Scriptures:

1. Acts 20:17-28. This passage uses a form of each of the three Greek words in reference to elders. Paul calls for the "elders (*presbuteroi*) of the church" at Ephesus (17). When they arrive, he addresses them (18-35) and charges them to "take heed to yourselves and to all the flock, among which the Holy Spirit has made you overseers (*episkopous*)" (28). Note that elders are addressed as overseers. Paul continues, saying to the elders, that they are "to shepherd (*poimainein*) the church of God." Elders, whom Paul calls "overseers," are instructed to "shepherd" the church. All three words are used in reference to the Ephesian elders. The New Testament makes no distinction among elders, presbyters, overseers, bishops, pastors and shepherds.[46] They are the same group of men addressed from the vantage points of their age (elders) and ministry performance (overseers that shepherd the church).

2. Titus 1:5-7. In setting forth the qualifications of each elder, Paul says he must be "blameless ... for a bishop must be blameless, as a steward of God." Paul tells us that elders are the bishops (overseers) of the local churches.

77

3. 1 Peter 5:1-2. Once again all three words are used in reference to elders: "The elders (*presbuterous*) who are among you I exhort ... Shepherd (*poimanate*) the flock of God which is among you, serving as overseers (*episkopountes*)." Peter agrees with Paul that elders, shepherds and overseers refer to the same ministry group.

4. Preachers are not pastors. The New Testament does not refer to its evangelists as pastors. The one verse in the English New Testament where the word *poimein* is translated "pastor" rather than "shepherd" makes a very clear distinction between evangelists (preachers) and pastors: "And he himself gave some to be apostles, some prophets, some evangelists, and some pastors and teachers" (Eph. 4:11). The ministries of pastor (elder) and preacher (evangelist) are clearly stated here as distinct. While preachers may also serve as elders (1 Peter 5:1) and while elders may also minister as preachers (1 Tim. 5:17), we cannot properly equate pastors (elders) with preachers (evangelists).

While some may view the local preacher as the pastor and an evangelist as a traveling preacher, the New Testament makes no such distinction. Paul had originally left Timothy, who was an evangelist (2 Tim. 4:5), in Ephesus for a special assignment. He instructs him to "remain in Ephesus" to accomplish the assignment (1 Tim. 1:3). Timothy had been located in Ephesus to do the work of an evangelist. He was not to travel from one place to the next in this evangelistic assignment, but remain at Ephesus until it was accomplished.

II. The Number of Elders Within a Local Church

When referring to the eldership of a local church, the New Testament always speaks of a plurality of elders. This is a distinguishing characteristic of the pattern followed by New Testament churches.

A. A Plurality of Elders is the Pattern for the Local Church

A plurality of elders was appointed for each of the churches in Derbe, Lystra, Iconium, and Pisidian Antioch (Acts 14;20-23). The Jerusalem church had a plural number of elders (Acts 15:2, 4, 6, 22) as did the church at Ephesus (Acts 20:17). The church at Philippi had "bishops and deacons" (Phil. 1:1). The church of the Thessalonians had a number of "those" that were "over" the church whose job it was to "see" to the proper conduct of the brethren. These were to be esteemed "very highly in love for their work's sake" (1 Thess. 5:12-15).

"Those" who were "over" the church are further defined in Hebrews 13:17: "Obey those who rule over you, and be submissive, for they watch out for your souls, as those who must give account." Paul leaves Titus in Crete to "set in order the things that are lacking, and appoint elders in every city as I commanded you" (Titus 1:5).[47]

The plurality of elders in each of these local churches is due to the teaching of the apostles who established them. There is no exception to this structure in the New Testament. This apostolic structuring of the local churches is a part of the pattern we are to "hold" (2 Tim. 1:13).

B. The Departure from this Order Was the Beginning of Apostasy

Paul foretold that from among the elders themselves men would arise speaking perverse things to draw away the disciples after them (Acts 20:28-31). The history of the church from the second century reveals that the departure from the apostles' pattern of a plurality of elders in a local church resulted in diocesan bishops over clusters of churches and finally in the papal bishop of Roman Catholicism.[48] There is no New Testament teaching or example for one bishop over the body of Christ, over several churches or even over a local church.

III. Local Church Autonomy

Contrary to the complex hierarchical system of one ruling bishop over many churches, the New Testament presents the autonomy of each local church, whether or not they have elders.

A. Definition

Autonomy is self-government. Local church autonomy means that each local church is self governing. This expresses the New Testament teaching that the government of each local church is limited to the boundaries of its own membership.

B. The Limit of Elders' Oversight

Paul's address to the elders of the church at Ephesus reveals that their oversight was limited to the Ephesian church. The fact that Paul called to him the elders of the church at Ephesus (Acts 20:17) points to the boundaries of that church as the limit of their oversight. When addressing them, Paul says, "Take heed to yourselves and to all the flock, among which the Holy Spirit has made you overseers" (Acts 20:28). Their oversight extended only to the church at Ephesus.

Peter's instruction to elders at large[49] lays a threefold stress on the limitation of the oversight of elders:

> The elders who are among you I exhort ... shepherd the flock of God which is among you, serving as overseers, not by constraint ... nor as being lords over those entrusted to you, but being examples to the flock (1 Peter 5:1-4).

1. "The flock of God which is among you." This restricts the oversight of elders to the flock, or local church, which they shepherd.

2. "Those entrusted to you." Those entrusted to these elders are the members of the local church "among" whom these elders served.

3. "Examples to the flock." It is only reasonable that the church have the example of their elders before them. No elder can be an example of a caring, helping shepherd if he is not available.

C. Local Autonomy in Churches With or Without Elders

The local churches in the New Testament are commended to the authority of the apostles' teaching (1 Cor. 4:17; 11:2;

7:17; 2 Thess. 2:15). Each church was independently responsible to maintain its own respect for the authority of God's Word.

1. The local church selected her own ministers (Acts 6:1-6). The apostles themselves delegated this autonomy.

2. The local church chose her own missionaries by the instruction of the Holy Spirit (Acts 13:1-3).

3. The local church was instructed to judge and discipline its own members (Matt. 18:17; 1 Cor. 5:1-13; 2 Thess. 3:6-15).

4. The local church was to settle its own internal problems (1 Cor. 6:1-5).

5. Each local church was responsible to respond to the Lord's instruction (Rev. 2:1-3:22). At the close of Christ's address to each of the seven local churches of Asia, all Christians were instructed to "hear what the Spirit says to the churches." Each church addressed was responsible to maintain her loyalties to Christ and to repent of her own failings. This is the pattern for all Christians and all local churches.

Earl Radmacher agrees:

> All "Church Government in the New Testament applies only to local bodies" ... The authority of the local church is final as far as its own affairs are concerned. (See Matt. 18:17). There is no higher court.[50]

The absence of any centralized earthly government among the churches of the New Testament and the responsibility of each local church to hold to the pattern of the apostles' teaching insist upon the autonomy of each local church. Local church autonomy is the safety valve against full-scale apostasy.

IV. Conclusion

In the organizational structure of the local church, a plurality of elders is appointed to oversee its affairs. The boundary of their oversight is limited to the membership of that local church. All churches are autonomous under the sovereign authority of Christ as expressed in the New Testament.

Quick-Answer Questions

1. Can you explain the meaning of the following terms as ministries in the local church: elder, pastor, shepherd?
2. What is the governmental structure of the universal church? the local church?
3. Do you perceive the distinction between the biblical view of a pastor and a denominational view of a pastor?
4. Comment on the practicality of local church autonomy as the safety valve against universal apostasy.

Discussion Questions

1. Explain from the Greek words in Acts 20:17, 28 and 1 Peter 5:1-2 that elders, overseers, pastors, shepherds are not different offices in the church but that all speak of the elders' ministry group.
2. Paul foresaw that the great apostasy that developed into ecclesiastical hierarchicalism would begin within the eldership (Acts 20:28-31). Why do you think the apostasy began in the eldership? What is necessarily inherent in the eldership that unscrupulous men desire?
3. Explain the fact that elders have an oversight authority within the local church after their appointment (Titus 1:5) that they did not have before the appointment. Comment on the essentiality of their oversight authority as requisite to fulfilling their appointed work.

CHAPTER 7

THE PASTORAL WORK AND QUALIFICATIONS OF ELDERS

By the time Paul wrote to Timothy at Ephesus, the eldership had made such a moral impact on the church that it had gathered to itself a proverbial expression: "If a man desires the position of a bishop, he desires a good work" (1 Tim. 3:1). Since the emphasis here is on the elder's work, Paul's next statements logically follow: "A bishop then must be" ... *qualified.* The purpose of this lesson is to define the biblical job description of elders and the essential qualifications that enable them to do their work.

The first two divisions of this lesson can be placed under two heads: BE and DO — that is, what elders must BE (qualified) and what they are subsequently qualified to DO (their work).

I. The Work of Elders (What They Must Do)

The work of elders, as stewards of God's precious flock, exceeds mere decision making. A knowledge of what their work actually embraces and its importance to the spiritual and emotional health of the members will result in an appreciation for the high qualifications required of each elder. The Bible states the relationship of the qualifications to the work as follows: "holding fast to the faithful word as he has been taught, that he may be able, by sound doctrine, both to exhort and to convict those who contradict" (Titus 1:9). The qualifications *enable* the elder to *do* his work. It seems reasonable, then, to consider elders' work before we study their qualifications.

A.   Elders Are Watchmen

Realizing that after his departure unscrupulous men, desirous of power, would attempt to exploit the authority of the Ephesian eldership, Paul charges them:

> Therefore take heed to yourselves and to all the flock, among which the Holy Spirit has made you overseers, to shepherd the church of God ... For I know that after my departure savage wolves will come in among you, not sparing the flock. Also from among yourselves men will rise up, speaking perverse things to draw away the disciples after themselves. Therefore *watch* ... (Acts 20:28-31).

Note the "Therefore *watch*." This same work assignment is attributed to the elders in Hebrews 13:17: "Obey those who rule over you, and be submissive, for they *watch* out for your souls, as those who must give account." Inherent in the term "watch" is the ancient responsibility of the watchmen of the city. Cities were protected by walls, and along the walls were watchtowers occupied by men who kept a vigilant eye for invaders. If an enemy were detected, the watchman would warn the city to prepare its defense. The security of the city was placed in the hands of the watchmen.

The job description of God's spiritual watchman is found in Ezekiel 3:16-21. Read the passage thoughtfully:

> ... the word of the Lord came to me, saying, Son of man, I have made you a watchman for the house of Israel; therefore hear a word from my mouth, and give them warning from me: When I say to the wicked, "You shall surely die," and you give him no warning, nor speak to warn the wicked from his wicked way, to save his life, that same wicked man shall die in his iniquity; but his blood will I require at your hand. Yet, if you warn the wicked, and he

does not turn from his wickedness, for his wicked way, he shall die in his iniquity; but you have delivered your soul. Again, when a righteous man turns from his righteousness and commits iniquity, and I lay a stumbling block before him, he shall die; because you did not give him warning, he shall die in his sin, and his righteousness which he has done shall not be remembered; but his blood will I require at your hand. Nevertheless, if you warn the righteous man that the righteous should not sin, and he does not sin, he shall surely live because he took warning; also you will have delivered your soul.

Notice that the job of the spiritual watchman is to warn the people with the Word of God. He fails to do so at the expense of his own soul! Thus the strength of the statement to the brethren that elders "watch out for your souls as they that must give account" (Heb. 13:17). Elders must warn the brethren with the Word of God against sinful errors and practices. This agrees with Paul's requirement that an elder must be "able to teach" (1 Tim. 3:2). No objective view of an elder as a watchman can interpret his teaching requirement to be less than a public teacher and protector standing between the Lord's people and those who would lead them astray.

B. Elders Shepherd the Flock (Acts 20:28; 1 Peter 5:1-3)

Notice the job of the elder is to "shepherd the church of God." This echoes the words of Christ that the shepherd having lost one sheep leaves the flock to search out the lost. Then finding it, he tenderly bears it upon his shoulders and returns with rejoicing to the sheepfold (Luke 15:3-7). The word "feed" in the older version is an unfortunate rendering because it has often been held to mean no more than to teach. However, the rendering "shepherd" embraces the entire spectrum of the elder's work of caring for the church (cf. 1 Tim. 3:4). The shepherd protects the flock, searches out the strays, binds up the broken limbs and feeds the sheep. And "the good shepherd gives his life for the sheep" (John 10:11). Those who will not so care for the flock are not shepherds, says the prophet (Ezek. 34:1-6).

C.   Elders Mature the Church (Eph. 4:11-16)

Included in Christ's "gifts" to the church, along with apostles, prophets, and evangelists, are "pastors" (shepherds). They are one of Christ's "gifts" to the local church. We know this embraces the local structure because pastors (elders) cannot scripturally exist outside the local church. The task of the shepherd is to bring spiritual children to maturity, that they may grow up, "no longer as children to be tossed to and fro by every wind of doctrine," but as spiritual adults standing secure in the faith and equipped for ministry, assuming their individual ministries in the body of Christ.

D.   Elders Personally Attend the Needs of Individual Members (1 Thess. 5:12-15)

Paul speaks of elders as those who are "over you in the Lord and admonish you" and instructs the church to "esteem them very highly in love for their work's sake." Their work includes warning the unruly, comforting the fainthearted, upholding the weak, and seeing that none render to anyone evil for evil.

The passage manifests a personal involvement in the private lives of needful brethren. Such cannot always be accomplished at a church service, or by a brief prayer at the end of a worship service. The true shepherd must genuinely care for newborn Christians whose lives may have just been shattered by some traumatic experience that may bring their trust in God to a crisis. It may require getting out of the church building, possibly into the homes and lives of Christ's precious children, putting a genuinely caring arm around an erring brother or sister and walking him or her or them through their problems to completion.

Leading the church to withdraw fellowship from the unfaithful is the very last resort. Every effort should first be made by personal contact to discover the hurt, the abuse, the source of the weakness, unfaithfulness or immorality and attempt a restoration of confidence in and faithfulness to Christ. The elder should employ the gentle encouragement of a loving spiritual father who knocks at the door of the heart, who cares for the wounded member, whose admonition is tender, understanding, patient, and above all healing.

We should underscore the phrase, "Esteem them very highly in love *for their work's sake*." The work of elders is by no means completed in a business meeting. Someone has observed that elders need not only head-power (knowledge of Scripture), and heart-power (sensitivity to human needs) but also *foot*-power. Their job description requires a personal involvement in the needs of members.

E. Elders Pray for the Sick (James 5:13-18)

The prayer of a godly man avails much. This passage does not seem to be speaking of the miraculous. James illustrates the power of the prayer of righteous men by the example of Elijah. By stating that Elijah was a man with a nature like ours today, he is surely saying that God will work through the prayers of righteous men even now.

Elijah prayed fervently to God seven times, each time sending his servant to observe any change in the weather and finally receiving an answer. The account in 1 Kings 18:41-46 notes that God did not grant the request immediately or miraculously. But interfering with the natural order while Elijah took the time to pray seven distinct prayers, God at last granted Elijah's request for rain. So will God answer the supplications of godly elders in behalf of the sick or in behalf of other matters, according to his will.

F. Elders Are Stewards of the Church of God (Titus 1:7)

Stewards take care of the goods of another for the benefit and joy of the owner. Elders should remember that they are stewards of God's precious flock. Paul said of stewards, "Moreover it is required in stewards that one be found faithful" (1 Cor. 4:2). They have a work assignment that extends

far beyond mere decision making to a wide range of requirements on their stewardship that are necessary to "take care of
the church of God" (1 Tim. 3:4). They are chosen on the basis of their qualifications and should be appointed with a sober
awareness that they will eventually give an account of themselves and of their charge to the owner (cf. Luke 16:1-2; Heb.
13:17).

G.   Restrictions While Doing the Work (1 Peter 5:1-4)

1. Not by constraint. A mere sense of duty devoid of heart
is not enough. Neither is serving reluctantly with the heart not
in it. A man must *desire* oversight (1 Tim. 3:1).

2. Not for dishonest gain. Elders can receive full support to work on a full time basis (1 Tim. 5:17- 18). This constitutes a warning not to exploit the eldership merely for a
livelihood. Such would mitigate the intended motive for service and could conceivably compromise the word of God and
the soundness of the oversight.

3. Not as being lords over those entrusted. Elders are
not to use their oversight authority to become dictators.
Authoritarianism is ruled out.

II. Qualifications of Elders (What They Must Be) (1 Tim. 3:1-7; Titus 1:5-9; 1 Peter 5:1-4)

These qualifications address the character, capabilities
and proper motivation of the elder essential to the success of
his ministry.[51] These qualifications are not merely to be located among the aggregate of the eldership, as if one elder can
be exempt from meeting a qualification if it is found in another. Paul clearly states that, "*A* bishop," that is, each bishop,
"then must be" qualified with each requirement.

The following recommends the different categories of
personal character, domestic relationships, social relationships,
teaching skills, doctrine and lifestyle under which the qualifications may be listed.

A. Negative Qualifications

1. Blameless, not open to censure, irreproachable.

2. Not given to wine, or not a brawler, not quarrelsome over wine.

3. Not violent, not a striker, a bruiser ready with a blow, pugnacious, contentious.

4. Not greedy for money, avaricious, eager for base gain, dishonest.

5. Not quarrelsome, not contentious.

6. Not covetous, no lover of money, not greedy, closed fisted, desirous of that which belongs to another.

7. Not a novice, a newly planted one, a new convert.

8. Not quick-tempered, not soon angry, prone to anger, short-fused and easy to ignite.

9. Not self-willed, one who wishes to have his way regardless of others.

B. Positive Qualifications

1. Husband of one wife, not an unmarried man. Each elder "must be" the husband of one wife. He must be a family man, or he would be without the experience Paul implies is necessary to "take care of the church of God" (1 Tim. 3:5).[52] Paul considers the home with its relationships to a wife and children as one of the principal considerations for qualifying a man for the ministry of oversight.

2. Temperate, sober, moderate.

3. Sober-minded, sensible.

4. Of good behavior, orderly.

5. Hospitable, generous to guests.

6. Able to teach, enabling him to both exhort in the sound doctrine and convict the gainsayers (cf. Titus 1:9). He should illustrate both ability as a teacher and a willingness to give himself to the preparation and the task of teaching.

7. A lover of what is good, that is, good men and/or good things.

8. Just, attempts to be fair in his judgments.

QUALIFICATIONS OF ELDERS

PERSONAL CHARACTER

NEGATIVE
not given to wine
not violent
not greedy for money
not quarrelsome
not covetous
not a novice
not self-willed
not quick-tempered
not (serving) by constraint
not for dishonest gain
not (serving) as lords
   over those entrusted

POSITIVE
blameless
temperate
sober-minded
good behavior
gentle
just
holy
self-controlled
holding to the word
a lover of what is good

DOMESTIC RELATIONSHIPS
husband of one wife
children in submission
not accused of:
   dissipation
   insubordination
rules his house well

SOCIAL RELATIONSHIPS/TEACHING SKILLS
hospitable
able to teach
good testimony among those outside

DOCTRINE/LIFESTYLE
holding fast the faithful word
examples to the flock

9. Holy, from *hosios* meaning a conduct that is observant of God's will.

10. Self-controlled, places a curb on himself; continent and content.

11. Holding fast the faithful word, which enables him to exhort and convict those that contradict (Titus 1:9).

12. Gentle, forbearing, as distinct from violent and quarrelsome.

13. A good testimony among those who are outside, has a good reputation from those who are not Christians.

14. Rules his own house well, with emphasis on "well," as opposed to authoritarianism or ruling with a heavy hand.

15. Having faithful children. Often it is insisted that the word "children" is plural and, therefore, the elder must have more than one child. But the Scripture also uses the word "children" in contexts where it is either meant or understood to include a single child. Consider the following:

a. 1 Timothy 5:4. "But if any widow has children or grandchildren, let them first learn to show piety at home and to repay their parents." Here the *children* and *grandchildren* are directed to care for *their* parents. If these "children" must be more than one child, that would seem to relieve an only child of this important obligation. Does not this passage include a widow with only one child?

b. 1 Timothy 5:16. "If any believing man or woman has widows, let them relieve them, and let not the church be burdened, that it may relieve those who are really widows." Here is a single man or woman that has plural *widows*. Must the "widows" be plural in number for the man or woman to be obligated to their care? Does not this include a man or a woman who has but a single widow?

c. Luke 14:26. "If anyone comes to me and does not hate his father and mother, wife and children, brothers and sisters, yes, and his own life also, he cannot be my disciple." Must the word "children" be more than one child? Does this not include families with a single child?

d. 1 Chronicles 2:30. "The sons of Nadab were Seled and

Appaim. Seled died without children." Does that mean Seled died without more than one child or that he died without any children at all? It is equivalent to saying that he died without a child.

e. *Genesis 21:7.* "She also said, Who would have said to Abraham that Sarah would nurse children? For I have born him a son in his old age." It is clear that Sarah had but one son, yet it was said that she nursed "children."

If you ask any gathering how many of them have children, those who have but one child will hold up their hand. It will happen every time. We must not be dogmatic about the number of children an elder must have, but is the child respectful, and if but a single child, is he or she a believer?

The qualifications of elders are not arbitrary. Through the years those men who strive to develop these character, domestic, doctrinal, social, and lifestyle traits also develop as a by-product a spirit that ennobles them and a moral expertise out of their experience that enables them to discharge their work of stewarding the church of God.

Paul's no-nonsense counsel to the Ephesian elders was to "take heed to yourselves and to all the flock," first to themselves, then to the flock (Acts 20:28). That's wise counsel for today.

III. The Relationship of the Local Church to the Eldership

A relationship of genuine respect for the elders is essential to the harmony, unity and spiritual development of the local church.

A. Esteem the Elders Exceeding Highly in Love (1 Thess. 5:12-13)

The by-product of a sincere effort to hold the elders in high estimation is to "be at peace among yourselves."

B. Be Submissive to the Elders (Heb. 13:17)

Cooperation with those who "watch out for your souls" is profitable for every member of the church and essential if they are to "do so with joy and not with grief."

C. Support Elders Who Devote Full Time to Their Work (1 Tim. 5:17-18)

The "double honor" includes both the esteem in which the "elders who rule well" are counted worthy and the "wages" they receive for full-time employment in their ministry. Paul quotes both Moses (Deut. 25:4) and Jesus (Luke 10:7) that any laborer "is worthy of his wages." How much worthier are those who labor for the church? This agrees with the principle laid out by Paul in 1 Corinthians 9:1-11 and Galatians 6:6.

D. Do Not Receive Accusations Against Elders (1 Tim. 5:19)

"... except from two or three witnesses." This is not a mere suggestion. It embraces good judgment as well as a commandment.

IV. Conclusion

The qualifications and work of elders can be placed under two heads: *be* and *do* — what elders "must be" in order that they may "do" the work. The gravity of that work is such that they will eventually "give account" of it to the Lord. The work of elders as overseers and spiritual shepherds requires their emotional, mental and physical resources. Sincere Christians who are attempting to cooperate with the Lord to bring about an ideal situation within a widely diversified group (the local church) can be grateful to God for structuring the local church with such men for such a ministry.

Quick-Answer Questions

1. Can you define the terms "elder," "overseer" and "pastor"?
2. Must each elder be fully qualified?
3. What is the "double honor" of 1 Timothy 5:17-18?

BE	AND	DO
QUALIFICATIONS →	enable elders to ——→	WORK
1 Timothy 3:1-7 Titus 1:5-9	Titus 1:9 Acts 20:31, Heb. 13:17	Exhort Convict Gainsayers Watch
POSITIVE	1 Thess. 5:12-15	Admonish the disorderly Encourage the fainthearted
AND		Support the weak
NEGATIVE	Eph. 4:11-16 James 5:14 Acts 20:28	Mature the saints Pray for the sick Shepherd the flock
	1 Timothy 3:5 Titus 1:7	Take care of the church as God's stewards

Discussion Questions

1. Give an illustration of the way elders' qualifications enable them to do their work.

2. Discuss the ministry of elders as stewards in behalf of God's church. For what and to whom shall they give account?

3. Discuss the ministry of elders as shepherds.

4. Discuss the relationship between the local church and the elders (cf. 1 Thess. 5:13-15). What attitude should members maintain toward unqualified elders? Answer from the principle in Matthew 23:1-3.

5. Elders are overseers. Explain from Scripture the extent of their oversight and the wisdom of its limitation.

6. What was the purpose of the watchman in antiquity? Describe the way elders serve the local church as watchmen? Use the language of Ezekiel 3:17.

7. With great respect for God's Word and the eldership, discuss the difference between the elders' oversight authority and authoritarianism.

CHAPTER 8

DEACONS

Another ministry in the local church is accomplished by men known as deacons. They are specially qualified for a special work. They are not mentioned in Ephesians 4:11-16 and, therefore, are not necessarily teachers. This lesson considers the significance of the term "deacons" and their work in the local church.

I. Definition and Significance of the Term

From the original, *diakonos*, deacon is more of a transliteration (bringing the sound over into the vernacular) than a translation.

A. Definition

1. Diakonos: Thayer's Lexicon defines *diakonos* as "one who executes the commands of another ... a servant, attendant, minister."[53] *Vine's Expository Dictionary* adds, "Whence English deacon, primarily denotes a servant, whether as doing servile work, or as an attendant rendering free service, without particular reference to its character."[54]

In the English New Testament the word is translated "minister," "servant" and "deacon." The word is "without particular reference to its character," that is, the word itself does not distinguish the *kind* of ministry or service to be performed. This can be illustrated by referring to Romans 12:6-7:

Having then gifts differing according to the grace that is given to us, let us use them: if prophecy, let us prophesy in proportion to our faith; or ministry, let us use it in our ministering.

The word "ministry" (*diakonia*) does not signify the *kind* of ministry or service to be performed. This can be illustrated in Colossians 4:17: "And say to Archippus, 'Take heed to the ministry which you have received in the Lord, that you may fulfill it.' " Since the term "ministry" does not convey the kind of ministry or service to be performed, we do not know the kind of ministry Archippus had received. Was he an elder, a deacon, a preacher, or had he received another ministry? We do not know.

The question arises, how then do translators know which word to translate for *diakonos*? Shall it be minister, servant, or deacon? The answer is from context.

B.   The Significance of the Word Deacon(s) in the Context of Philippians 1:1 and 1 Timothy 3:8-13

"Paul, and Timothy, servants of Jesus Christ, to all the saints in Christ Jesus who are in Philippi, with the bishops and deacons" (Phil. 1:1).

Why is the word *diakonos* rendered "deacons" when "ministers" or "servants" would be a correct translation? All of God's people are servants, ministers. But in this context these *diakonos* are separately addressed from the rest of the saints and are therefore distinguished from them. They are also mentioned together with the bishops. In this context both the *diakonos* and the overseers are distinguished from the rest of the saints in the opening address. We also know from 1 Timothy 3 that both elders/bishops and *diakonos*/deacons are distinguished from other servants of God by their special qualifications. We know that all Christians do not have to meet the qualifications of 1 Timothy 3:8-13 (such as being the husband of one wife) to be servants or ministers of Christ. Therefore, these *diakonos* are translated deacons rather than ministers or servants to distinguish their special ministry for which they are specially prepared.

II. The Work of Deacons

There is no description in the New Testament of the work of deacons as there is of elders. Their work must be determined from the verb *diakoneo* – to serve, wait upon, minister – and from the context in which the word is used.

A. Qualifications and Work of Special Servants in Acts 6:1-6

This passage details the ministry of specially qualified servants. While the noun *diakonos* is not used, other forms of the word are used in a context that implies a special need for specially qualified men for a special *service (diakonia)*. During the beginnings of the church, when it was rapidly growing, some of the widows among the Hellenists[55] "were neglected in the daily distribution (*diakonia*)" (Acts 6:1-2). To provide these widows' needs and at the same time relieve the apostles of concern so they could continue in their ministry of preaching and prayer, seven specially qualified men were appointed to "serve" (*diakonein*) the widows' tables. Thus being specially qualified for special service in the local church, we can refer to these special servants as deacons as correctly as the servants in Philippians 1:1 and 1 Timothy 3:8-13.

Note that there are two ministries mentioned in this context: "the ministry (*diakonia*) of the word" (v. 4) and the ministry of serving (*diakonein*) tables (v. 2). The importance of these special servants and their special ministry is highlighted in the following:

1. A business to be accomplished (v. 3).

2. Qualifications to be met (v. 2).

3. An appointment to be made (vv. 3, 5-6). This may be the occasion of the origin of deacons in the local church.

B. Purpose of Deacons

It seems from the context of Acts 6:1-6 and the meaning of the word *diakonos*, servant, that deacons' special work should be relieving the church of any burden needing attention so that it can function effectively in evangelism and the maturing ministries of the local church. If this is true, then deacons have a wide range of activity. Good men who prove well qualified for the their particular tasks should be selected and given the authority to function in that area of work.

C. Upshot of the Appointment of Deacons

The result of the appointment of these special servants at Jerusalem was that "the word of God spread, and the number of the disciples multiplied greatly in Jerusalem, and a great many of the priests were obedient to the faith" (Acts 6:7). The multiplying of the disciples by evangelism was the occasion of the neglect of the widows in the church at Jerusalem (v. 1) and could have been the occasion for distracting the leadership away from their ministry of evangelism. But the appointment of these special servants released the preachers to their ministry, and the church continued to grow from without while simultaneously her internal needs were cared for.

This illustrates how God has wisely structured the local church for fruitful ministry.

III. Qualifications of Deacons (1 Tim. 3:8-13)

A. Negative

1. Not double-tongued, saying one thing to one person and a different thing to another.

2. Not given (addicted) to wine. At a time when little water was used because of health reasons, wine was used for drinking purposes.

3. Not greedy for money.

B. Positive

1. Reverent, "men of dignity" (NASB), "worthy of respect" (NIV).

2. Holding the mystery of the faith with a pure conscience. A part of God's mystery from eternity was that the Gentiles would be fellow partakers with the Israelites in all the promised messianic blessings of redemption and privilege (Eph. 3:3-6). This mystery was revealed in the proclamation of the gospel to *all* men. Some Jews apparently had a hard time with this and could have been prejudiced against Gentiles and the idea that they stood equal before God with the Jews. Also Gentiles could have been prejudiced toward the Jews (Rom. 11:11-22). In order to serve all members of the local church with equal care deacons had to be without prejudice.

3. The husband of one wife.

4. Ruling their children and houses well, with emphasis on "well."

C.   They Are First to Be Proved

A reasonable period of time is required to know a person and his capabilities. Perhaps this refers to a period of testing wherein deacons' assignments are to be discharged before appointing them deacons.

IV. Deaconesses in the Early Church?

The idea of deaconesses in the apostolic church is not new. Some have sincerely thought deaconesses are the specially qualified "women" of 1 Timothy 3:11, correctly translated "wives" in the NKJV and NIV. Others have thought the RSV is correct in translating Romans 16:1, "I commend to you our sister Phoebe, a *deaconess* of the church at Cenchreae." But is there any scriptural evidence to justify either this translation of Romans or the interpretation of the "women" in 1 Timothy 3:11 as deaconesses?

The following will show that the idea of deaconesses in the early church is untenable.

A.   Disrupting the Unity of 1 Timothy 3:8-13

To interpret (not translate) the "women" of 1 Timothy 3:11 as deaconesses disrupts the unity of the context because 1 Timothy 3:8-13 is clearly a statement of the qualifications of deacons. Viewing these "women" as deaconesses has Paul interrupting the context to insert the qualifications of deaconesses in verse 11 after listing only half the qualifications of deacons in verses 8-10, then returning to complete the qualifications of deacons in verses 12-13. Such a disruption of the context is confusing as well as without good reason.

B. A Translation Preferred over an Interpretation

The word "women" is *gunaikas*, which can be translated either "wives" or "women." The singular *gune* can be translated either "wife" or "woman." It is, therefore, very important to understand that the translator's choice of the word is often dependent on the context. Since the context of 1 Timothy 3:8-13 is a statement of the qualifications of deacons, it is correct and consistent with the context to translate *gunaikas* in 1 Timothy 3:11 "wives." One of the qualifications of deacons, then, is that their wives must be "reverent, not slanderers, temperate, faithful in all things." These qualifications are appropriately applied to the wives of deacons who also must attain a high quality of Christian character in order for their husbands to be fully qualified as deacons. This *translation* makes it clear that verse 11 states another qualification of deacons and keeps the unity of the context. "Wives" as a *translation* is preferred over an *interpretation* that views these *gunaikas* as deaconesses.

Since the New Testament is without any evidence for deaconesses, the translation of the RSV is without adequate justification either linguistically or scripturally for its translation of "deaconesses" in Romans 16:1.

C. No Clear Statement of Deaconesses in the New Testament

Until we have a clear statement from the text that there were deaconesses in the early church, we are without divine authority to have them. Is it possible that the later innovation of deaconesses into the organization of the local church has been read back into Scripture as justification for the practice? Respect for the authority of Scripture will hardly allow that when there is an attempt to restore the New Testament pattern to the modern church.

V. Conclusion

A church with good deacons, who relieve evangelists, shepherds and teachers to do their work, makes a more fruitful church. Those deacons who serve well earn themselves a good report. Deacons, however, are not junior elders. Their ministry is distinct from elders. Perhaps knowledgeable deacons would thereby receive from the elders their best report.

Quick-Answer Questions

1. The word *diakonos* can be translated "minister" or "servant." In Philippians 1:1 and 1 Timothy 3:8- 13 it is translated "deacon." Why was this translation selected?
2. What is the meaning of the word "deacon"?
3. Does the word "servant" or "minister" distinguish the kind of service or ministry to be performed? How, then, can we tell from Scripture what service or ministry a servant or a minister is to perform? Will another look at Colossians 4:17 help?

Discussion Questions

1. It seems the original occasion for instituting deacons in the church is described in Acts 6:1-6. On what other scriptural grounds do we come to that conclusion?
2. Identify the two ministries mentioned in Acts 6:1-6. Then discuss how the appointment of the seven relieved the apostles to their particular ministry. Does Acts 6:7 reflect on the success of the appointment in the Jerusalem church? In what way?

CHAPTER 9

EVANGELISTS

Essential to spreading the borders of the kingdom are the evangelists of the church, for "How shall they believe in him of whom they have not heard? And how shall they hear without a preacher?" (Rom. 10:14). Evangelists are also listed among the "gifts" Christ gave for the spiritual growth and development of the local church (Eph. 4:11-14). In God's spiritual economy the evangelist is assigned an important role in both the universal and the local church. This lesson considers the meaning of the terms "evangelist" and "preacher," his work, his essential qualities and his support.

I.   Definitions

The following terms will help define what a preacher is and the preacher's biblical job description.

A.   Evangelist

From *euangelistes*, "a bringer of good tidings, an evangelist...this name is given in the New Testament to those heralds of salvation through Christ who are not apostles: Acts 21:8; Eph. 4:11; 2 Tim. 4:5."[56] This term "evangelist" (*euangelistes*) comes from *euangelion* which is translated "gospel." Since the gospel is the good news message and the evangelist is the bringer of that message, an evangelist is actually a "gospelizer," a bringer of the good news message of salvation by grace through faith in Christ Jesus.

B.   Preacher

Vine states that *kerux*, "a herald, is used of the preacher of the gospel, 1 Tim. 2:7; 2 Tim. 1:11 ... indicates the preacher as giving a proclamation."[57] Thayer defines it as "a herald, a messenger vested with public authority, who conveyed the official messages of kings, magistrates, princes, military commanders, or who gave a public summons or demand."[58]

C.   Preach

Thayer states that *kerusso*, the verb form of *kerux*, means "to be a herald, to officiate as a herald, to proclaim after the manner of a herald; always with a suggestion of formality, gravity, and an authority which must be listened to and obeyed."[59] Paul encouraged Timothy to "preach the word" (2 Tim. 4:2), to proclaim the message as a herald with the authority of Christ.

D.   The Prophets and the Preacher

The Old Testament prophets were kindred spirits with the preachers in the New Testament in passionate delivery and content of their message. Far from being mere foretellers, the prophets were speakers for God, speaking the message God gave them whether it related to the past, present or future.

The biblical definition of a prophet is a "mouth, a spokesman" (Ex. 4:15-16). Moses stated that the function of the prophet was to speak just that word God placed in his mouth (Deut. 18:17-19). When God called Jeremiah to be his prophet, the young man shrank back, fearing he could not measure up to the task. Recognizing that the prophet was a speaker for God, he replied, "Ah, Lord God! Behold, I cannot speak, for I am a youth" (Jer. 1:6). But God replied, "Do not say, I am a youth .... Whatever I command you, you shall speak.... Behold, I have put my words in your mouth" (Jer. 1:7, 9). The historian later wrote that Jeremiah "spoke from the mouth of the Lord" (2 Chron. 36:12).

The prophet, then, was God's spokesman, God's mouth. He was also God's *messenger*. As expressed by another: "Then

Haggai, the Lord's messenger, spoke the Lord's message to the people" (Hag. 1:13). The prophets were God's spokesmen, God's mouths, God's messengers. As such they were much more than foretellers; they were *forthtellers*, speaking forth the word that God had placed in their mouths.

In New Testament times the man who used his capabilities of speech to convey the message of kings, magistrates, princes and military commanders was called a *kerux*. His task was to speak the message of the king to the people, to deliver messages from the military commander to the tribune in the field. In the New Testament the word *kerux* is translated "preacher." It is very appropriate for the Holy Spirit to call him who proclaims the Lord's message a *kerux*, a preacher. He is God's messenger to herald the message of the Lord, the message of good news that sinful man can be justified and saved by God's grace through faith in Christ. Thus, the task of the gospel preacher is the same as the prophet's task: to proclaim the message revealed by God. The work of one is the work of the other: preach the word!

The only difference between the ancient prophet and the modern preacher is the method by which the message is received. The prophet received his message by revelation and preached it by inspiration; the modern preacher obtains his message from the Scriptures and preaches it by diligent preparation and prayer. The preacher is to get God's message from Scripture and preach *that* message to the people. In this way the preacher today is God's mouth, God's messenger, his *kerux*.

II. The Work of an Evangelist

Paul charged Timothy to "do the work of an evangelist, fulfill your ministry" (2 Tim. 4:5). The statement discloses that both Paul and Timothy recognized there was a distinctive job description that constituted the preacher's ministry and that Paul expected Timothy to "fulfill" it. The following seeks to set forth the work of an evangelist in ascending levels of requirement of knowledge, of ministry experience and of consequent capability.

A. Preach the Word — Evangelize (2 Tim. 4:2,5)

The definitions of the words "evangelist" and "preacher" convey an important part of the preacher's work. An evangelist proclaims the glad tidings of salvation to the lost. A local evangelist, like Timothy at Ephesus, has an assigned task of preaching the word of God to the church (see 1 Tim. 4:6, 11-16). But a primary work of the gospel preacher is evangelism, soul winning, proclaiming the good news to the lost. No evangelist fulfills his ministry by confining his work to the pulpit. An evangelist will intentionally seek to save the lost. When looking for a preacher, a local church should list soul winning as a priority requirement.

B. Edify the Local Church (Eph. 4:11-16)

Local preaching includes equipping the members for ministry, bringing the members to the unity of the faith and to the knowledge of Christ and bringing spiritual children to spiritual maturity while stabilizing them against the winds of error. The preacher's job of edifying the church (building up the body) begins with putting the brethren in mind of the apostles' ways (1 Cor. 4:17). God intends for his people to be built up by public proclamation and teaching (1 Tim. 4:6-16). Paul charged the preacher: "Take heed to yourself and to the doctrine. Continue in them, for in doing this you will save both yourself and those who hear you" (v. 16). Feeling the pulse of the local membership and supplying their needs require a bit more knowledge and experience than that required to lead souls to Christ.

C. Appoint Elders (Titus 1:5)

God wants elders in every church. No local church is fully structured to meet the spiritual needs of its members until qualified elders are in place. A work of the local preacher is to appoint elders in every church without them and to maintain a qualified eldership in every church where they exist. From the initial effort to the final appointment of an eldership can take years. This requires a bit more wisdom and experience and often great patience to see one's efforts emerge at last into reality.

The word "appoint" carries the idea of an appointment to administer an office. Appointing elders is "not a formal ecclesiastical ordination ... but the appointment for the recognition of the churches, of those who had already been raised up and qualified by the Holy Spirit, and had given evidence of this in their life and service."[60] In other words, the churches selected and approved the men to be appointed.

This is illustrated in Acts 6:1-6 where the church was instructed to choose from among themselves seven qualified men for a task to which the apostles would then appoint them. The appointment of the seven men by the apostles was carried out with the approval of the church who actually selected them.

This idea carries over into the appointment of the elders by Paul and Barnabas in each of the Galatian churches (Acts 14:23). When Paul and Barnabas "appointed elders in every church," it was done with the churches' approval of those men who had evidenced their gifts from God to discharge the work of elders. This same idea is expressed in 2 Corinthians 8:16-19 where a praiseworthy brother was "appointed (not by voting, but with general approbation) by the churches in Greece to accompany the apostle in conveying their gifts to the poor saints in Judea."[61] Thus the Holy Spirit makes elders (Acts 20:28), the church selects them and an evangelist or someone else appoints them with the general approval of the church.

The idea of Titus appointing elders by the selection and approval of the church is to be distinguished from the claim that the local preacher has "evangelistic authority" over the local church and thus has the authority to appoint elders of his own selection. This latter idea has been further stretched to mean that since the evangelist has authority to select and appoint elders of his own choice, he, therefore, has authority over the elders he appoints. However, the only authority the evangelist has is the authority of the word of God (cf. 1 Tim. 4:11; Titus 2:15). The "things" he is commanded to teach with all authority are the "these things" mentioned in God's Word.

Through preaching, teaching and prayer, the evangelist assists the local church to mature, select and appoint elders.

D. Defend the Faith (1 Tim. 1:3; 6:20-21; Titus 1:10-13; 2 Tim. 4 :1-5)

This is not the choicest part of the preacher's work, but it is often necessary. From the beginning, men have challenged the existence of God and the doctrine of creation, the inspiration and authority of the Scriptures, the deity of Christ, the resurrection and the truth of the gospel. In the past three and a half centuries, a denominationalized view of Christianity has challenged the Bible's teaching about the unity of the church, the identity of the church, its organizational structure, the design and purpose of baptism, the authority of Scripture and the place of women in leadership. History will show that, in the main, it was gospel preachers, sound in doctrine and possessed of strong convictions, who stood for the truth and preserved the church against error. Only constant prayer and pouring over the Scriptures can enable the evangelist to identify and defeat the crafters of false doctrine and to expose the violations of the pattern of sound words. Paul exhorted the preacher:

> I charge you therefore before God and the Lord Jesus Christ ... Preach the word! Be ready in season and out of season. Convince, rebuke, exhort, with all longsuffering and teaching. For the time will come when they will not endure the sound doctrine, but according to their own desires, because they have itching ears, they will heap up for themselves teachers, and they will turn their ears away from the truth, and turn aside to fables. But you be watchful in all things, endure afflictions, do the work of an evangelist, fulfill your ministry (2 Tim. 4:1-5).

This work requires of the preacher a doctrinal expertise that is never ending in prayer, Bible study and research.

E. Train Preachers and Teachers (2 Tim. 2:2)

"And the things that you have heard from me among many witnesses, commit these to faithful men who will be able to teach others also."

Luke mentions Timothy's early experience in preacher training as an on-the-field apprentice under the direct supervision of the apostle Paul and something of the success of their combined efforts (Acts 16:1-5). Later Luke records Paul training in a more formal atmosphere for two years in the school of Tyrannus and the successful results of that arrangement (Acts 19:9-10). Years later, in his final letter, Paul passes the torch on to Timothy to do the work of preacher-teacher training (2 Tim. 2:2). Whether a Timothy-Paul method or a full academic arrangement, preacher-teacher training is the work of the preacher, says Paul. The future of the church depends on it, for "the harvest truly is plentiful, but the laborers are few" (Matt. 9:37). This will require more of the practical experience of a veteran preacher.

Perhaps it would be well for local preachers to evaluate their ministry in light of an evangelist's job-description as outlined above and make a ministry judgment about whether they are actually engaged in doing "the work of an evangelist."

III. Qualities of an Evangelist

The term "man of God" is used in the Bible only of Old Testament prophets and of New Testament preachers (1 Tim. 6:11; 2 Tim. 3:16). Such terminology, expressing whose man the preacher really is, would have to be accompanied by certain godly qualities for an effective preaching ministry.

A.   Is an Example to the Believers

"Let no one despise your youth, but be an example to the believers in word, in conduct, in love, in spirit, in faith, in purity" (1 Tim. 4:12).

No one despises a young preacher merely because he is young, but only if his conduct and/or his preaching do not match his job assignment. The same can be said for preachers of any age.

B.   Completely Given to the Work, Diligent (1 Tim. 4:15; 2 Tim. 2:15)

Most likely the reference in 2 Timothy 2:15 does not

mean to study the Bible. The rendering in the King James Version, "Study to shew thyself approved unto God," employs archaic English terms with meanings now out of touch with the modern vernacular. The New King James version better translates, "Be diligent to present yourself approved to God, a worker who does not need to be ashamed." This clarifies Paul's meaning that the evangelist is to be diligent in *all* phases of his ministry. A lazy preacher is a liability to the local church, but a diligent worker will have no reason to be ashamed before God or men. Rather, his progress will be evident to all.

C. Takes Heed to Himself and to His Doctrine (1 Tim. 4:16)

Taking heed to oneself likely pertains to the Christian character of which the evangelist is to be an example (as mentioned in 1 Tim. 4:12), as well as the pure motivations which are the driving forces of his ministry. Paul gave this same exhortation to the Ephesian elders (Acts 20:28). Personal spiritual development seems to be primary on Paul's list of requirements for effective Christian leadership. Also the preacher must continue his Scripture studies with a view toward matching his doctrine with the Bible's teaching. An objective mind and a heart gratefully dedicated to Christ and continual prayer for more accurate understanding of revealed truth will surely achieve Paul's intention in this instruction.

D. Manifests Urgency in Preaching (2 Tim. 4:2)

Christ's death and resurrection and his promise to return with both salvation and judgment have implications upon the human race toward which God's man can never become detached and dispassionate. Hence, he is always ready to preach the word, in season and out.

E. Is Gentle, an Able Teacher, Patient, Humble (2 Tim. 2:24-26)

In context these qualities do not identify with an attack mentality that would consume an individual who may be slightly to the right or left of a minor point of doctrine. On the contrary, "a servant of the Lord must not quarrel but be gentle to all, able to teach, patient, in humility correcting those who are in opposition, if God perhaps will grant them repentance, so that they may know the truth, and that they may come to their senses and escape the snare of the devil."

In summary, God's man will be steadfast in the faith, loyal to the truth, refusing false and speculative doctrines and uncompromising toward error. At the same time he will conduct himself in a manner that is gentle, patient and humble rather than quarrelsome. He will manifest the kind of loving spirit that says he genuinely cares about the *person* who is in opposition to himself.

IV. Their Support

The right to be supported by those whom the evangelist serves is the clear teaching of Scripture.

A. The Principle and the Commandment (Rom. 15:27; 1 Cor. 9:1-14)

While gathering famine relief money for Jewish brethren, Paul said, "If Gentiles have been partakers of their spiritual things, their duty is also to minister to them in material things" (Rom. 15:27). A debt to the one who has preached the gospel is actually incurred by the one who receives the gospel. In 1 Corinthians 9 Paul speaks of the "right" of gospel preachers to receive support from the brethren (vv. 4-6,12), and sets forth several examples in which men rightfully partake of the fruit of their labors. From this he draws a principle, "If we have sown spiritual things for you, is it a great thing if we reap your material things?" (v. 11). Then building on the principle, he concludes, "Even so the Lord has commanded that those who preach the gospel should live from the gospel" (v. 14).

B. Churches Are Obligated to Support Their Evangelists (Gal. 6:6-10; cf. 2 Cor. 11:7-8; Phil. 4:10-20)

1. Sharing with the teacher. From the original, *koinonia*, comes the words "fellowship," "participate" and "share."

It is rendered "contribution" (Rom. 15:26), "communion" (1 Cor. 10:16; 2 Cor. 13:14), "fellowship" (1 Cor. 10:20), and "share" (Gal. 6:6; Heb. 13:16). In each case it means to participate.

In the Galatians passage Paul illustrates that you get what you pay for by appealing to the law of sowing and reaping. Perhaps some needed to be reminded, then as now, of the fundamental axiom that if you sow abundantly, you reap abundantly, and if you sow sparingly, you will reap sparingly. The idea seems to be that if brethren hold back and do not share their monetary gain with their teacher(s), they are sowing to their flesh. Even as flesh dies, so will they spiritually. If the preacher must work to support himself, he is deprived of precious time for prayer and study essential to preparation.

God is not mocked in either nature or the church. Spiritual law is as immutable as natural law. To sow wheat seed is to reap wheat. To sow the word is to reap a spiritual harvest. To sow abundantly is to reap abundantly. To support a diligent, conscientious evangelist is to experience a return in spiritual benefits.

The individual can have fellowship with the teacher through the local church as did the Philippians (Gal. 6:6; Phil. 4:15-16).

2. Support of other workers (Titus 3:13-14; 3 John 5-8).
The principle to which Paul appeals for the support of the preachers extends to all who would labor for the church in full or part-time capacity.

V. Clergy and Laity?

We read of no special titles for preachers in the New Testament. Jesus cautioned spiritual leaders against the desire for special titles that are accompanied by special privilege (Matt. 23:1-10). The preacher who remembers that he is saved by grace and is a servant of the church will not put a gap between the pulpit and the pew.

An interesting note is found in two Scriptures that speak of God's clergy and laity. Ephesians 1:11 says that all who are in Christ "were made a heritage."[62] The word "heritage" is from *kleroo*, the word from which "clergy" was derived. But the Scripture is clear that it is God's people who are the heritage (clergy). The second Scripture is 1 Peter 2:9 that refers to God's "holy people." The Greek word for "people" is *laos*, from which is derived the term "laity." Both laity and clergy are God's people. There is no distinction between God's clergy and God's laity. Such terms should never have been employed to make such an unchristian distinction.

Perhaps, however, there is a special designation, though it may be too great for some to wear properly. One day the Lord will call each of the redeemed by that designation when he welcomes us home, "Well done, thou good and faithful *servant*."

VI. Conclusion

Evangelists are a very important part of the ministry that God has designed for the local church. God wants his word preached to the local church as well as to the lost world. Without the proclamation of the Word, the church will lose her hold on the faith and, consequently, will lose her identity. Evangelists are an indispensable part of the church's world mission. Preaching is an indispensable part of God's design for the maturing of the local church.

Quick-Answer Questions

1. Define the meaning of the words "evangelist" and "preacher."
2. What is the five-fold biblical job description of an evangelist?
3. What is Paul's meaning to "preach the word"?

Discussion Questions

1. There are no inspired preachers today, but the function of gospel preachers is the same as the Bible prophets. Analyze this function.

2. Define the work of a *kerux*. Then tell what the content of the preacher's message should be.

3. Some think preaching has a minimal effect on lifestyle changes. Some think preaching should be reduced or even replaced. Would this kind of attitude be more likely to reflect Bible teaching or poor preaching?

4. Since the word "ordain" or "appoint," as used in Titus 1:5, means an appointment by general approbation, explain how the evangelist appoints elders.

5. If an church does not support an evangelist full time, can that church suffer? Explain.

PART THREE

THE WORK AND WORSHIP OF THE CHURCH

In response to the preaching of Peter and the other Apostles, 3,000 "received the word gladly," were baptized and added unto them "that day" (Acts 2:14, 41). A little later this church had grown to 5,000 (Acts 4:4). It is clear that the believers acted as a corporate unit. They had a definite doctrinal standard (Acts 2:42); they had fellowship with one another as believers; they observed the ordinances of baptism and the Lord's supper (vss. 42-47); they met for public worship (vs. 46); and they contributed to the support of the needy (vss. 44,45). Surely, we have here the marks of an organized local church, even if the organization was only loose as yet.

Earl D. Radmacher quoting Henry Clarence Thiessen, from *What the Church is All About*, p. 321.

CHAPTER 10

THE WORK OF THE CHURCH

Someone has observed that Christ did not take us straight from the baptistry to heaven because he has a work for us to do. That observation seems true. This lesson considers what that work is and God's design for it to be accomplished within the framework of the local church.

I. Glory to God in the Church

Jesus said, "By this my Father is glorified, that you bear much fruit" (John 15:8). Paul wrote, "Now to him who is able to do exceedingly abundantly above all that we ask or think, according to the power that works in us, to him be the glory in the church by Christ Jesus throughout all ages, world without end. Amen" (Eph. 3:20-21). Clearly God's purpose is for his people to glorify him in the church by bearing much fruit. That fruit is borne through the work of the church.

II. The Work of the Church

The work of the church is evangelism, edification (encouraging and maturing the members), relief, discipline and restitution of weak and erring members.

A. The Work of Evangelism

From *euangelion* comes "good news," "glad tidings," or the preeminent New Testament translation, "gospel." From *eu-*

angelistes is the word "evangelist." Hence an evangelist is actually a "gospelizer," a bringer of the gospel of Christ. To evangelize, then, means to announce glad tidings or to preach the gospel. "Gospel" is used of the good tidings of the coming kingdom (Mark 1:14-15). It is also used of the good news that God saves by grace through faith in Christ (Rom. 1:16). Again, it is used of the good news that the Old Testament prophets foresaw and that was first "reported" or "announced" to the world by Spirit-guided gospel preachers (1 Peter 1:10-12). Hence evangelism is the work of preaching the gospel to the lost, of bringing the good news message of justification by faith in Christ to the world of lost men.

1. The great commission (Matt. 28:18-20; Mark 16:15-16). Here is the commission to disciple all nations, to preach the gospel to all creation. Those discipled and baptized are to teach others in turn. Jesus tells us that preaching the gospel is the work of the church that was foretold in the Old Testament Scriptures (Luke 24:44-47). This is the work for which Jesus pledged to exercise his authoritative presence with us "even to the end of the age."

All Christians are embraced in this commission. Peter wrote that Christians are "a chosen generation, a royal priesthood, a holy nation, his own special people, that you may proclaim the praises of him who called you out of darkness into his marvelous light" (1 Peter 2:9). Here is a statement of being and a statement of purpose. God made us to be a certain kind of people to fulfill a special purpose, the purpose of proclaiming the praises of God!

From *exangello* comes the word "proclaim." Its literal meaning is to tell out, to proclaim abroad, to publish completely. This speaks to every Christian as these quotations from different versions of the Bible will show. God called us out of darkness and made us to be his own possession to "*declare* the praises of him" (NIV), to "*declare* the wonderful deeds of him" (RSV), "that ye may *proclaim* the excellencies of him" (NASB), "that you may *proclaim* the perfections of him" (New Catholic Edition), "to *tell* about the wonderful things he has done" (The Everyday Bible), "to *proclaim* the wonderful acts of God" (Good News For Modern Man), "that you may *declare* the virtues of him" (Goodspeed's translation), "it is your task to *proclaim* the noble deeds of him" (Barclay's translation), "that you may *make known* the perfections of him (Weymouth's translation), "that you should *declare* the perfections of him who has called you from darkness into his marvelous light" (translation by Doctors George Campbell, James Macknight, and Philip Doddridge).

Without controversy all Christians sustain some relationship to God's purpose for calling us out of the world's darkness into his redemptive light – the work of telling others about what God has done for us through our Lord Jesus Christ. This is the great work for all those called out of darkness.

2. Accomplished by the apostles. The Holy Spirit testifies that in obedience to Christ, the apostles "went out and preached everywhere" (Mark 16:15-20). Luke caught the evangelistic spirit of the apostles when he said, "Daily in the temple, and in every house, they did not cease preaching and teaching Jesus as the Christ" (Acts 5:42). It was said of the apostles that they "turned the world upside down" (Acts 17:6).

3. Accomplished by the early church. The apostles were soon joined by the rest of the members of the church in their evangelistic mission. Luke says that after the apostles reported "to their own company" the threats of the ruling Jews in Jerusalem, the church prayed for boldness to speak, "and they were all filled with the Holy Spirit, and they spoke the word of God with boldness" (Acts 4:23-31). The persecution that soon scattered the church away from Jerusalem only fired their evangelistic zeal, for "those who were scattered went everywhere preaching the word" (Acts 8:4). See also Acts 11:19-26; 15:35; 19:9-10; and 1 Thess. 1:8. Evangelism is indeed the great work of the church.

B. The Work of Edification (Eph. 4:11-16)

An edifice is a house, and the word "edification" originally meant "building a house." Here it is used of building a house within, of building up the Christian's spiritual house, of promoting spiritual growth. Edification is one of the major purposes for the church assembling regularly (1 Cor. 14:26). Paul says that one of the evangelist's jobs is edification, building up the body of Christ. This is a major reason that Christ gave special gifts of evangelists, shepherds and teachers, the gifts of leadership to the local churches.

Edification begins where evangelism ends. It is the work of maturing spiritual babes so that they may "come to the unity of the faith," that they "no longer be children, tossed to and fro and carried about with every wind of doctrine," but "speaking the truth in love, may grow up in all things into him who is the head – Christ." Edification begins with an education of both a doctrinal and practical sort in order to mature. Christ wants every new Christian to "grow up" spiritually. This is an important job assignment for the leadership of the local church.

C. The Work of Relieving Those in Need (1 Tim. 5:16)

An important work of the church is the relief of physical needs, as in the case of the widows at Jerusalem in Acts 6:1-6. The early church was very zealous in this regard as seen in the following passages: Acts 2:44-45; 4:32-37; 6:1-6; 11:27-30; Rom. 15:26-27; 2 Cor. 8:1-9:15; Gal. 2:10; 1 Tim. 5:1-16; James 1:27. In this particular work the church today seems everywhere characterized by a generous spirit of compassion to the distress and needs of others.

D. The Work of Discipline and Restitution

The church is further instructed in the work of restoring weak and fallen members to Christ (Gal. 6:1-5; James 5:19-20) and in the final act of disciplining those who err in doctrine or life but refuse repentance and restitution (Matt. 18:15-17; 1 Cor. 5:1-13; 2 Thess. 3:6-15). The Lord's loving reminder is that those who are spiritual are to restore these wounded brothers and sisters "in a spirit of gentleness" (Gal. 6:1; 2 Tim. 2:24-26) because the ultimate purpose of such discipline is to save those precious souls for whom Christ died (1 Cor. 5:5).

III. The Organized Local Church

The church is not pictured in th New Testament as an un-orginized mass of floating members, without local church membership and responsibilities to its program of work. The following presents the local churches with their qualified leaderships as support bases for spiritual growth and development, for healing of the wounded, for strengthening the faint and weakened, for encouragement and edification in Christ, for direction into evangelism and caring for those in need.

A. Organized Local Churches Seen Throughout the New Testament

The body of Christ throughout the New Testament is presented as having a distinct structure that is designed to expedite the church's mission. The picture that emerges is of local congregations that are autonomous, that at the final level of development are structured with a qualified leadership to provide spiritual oversight into the mission of the church. New converts are not left to wander aimlessly. Local churches are organized units of God's people into which new Christians are to be lovingly guided into worship, work, and spiritual growth. A local church is a unit of the divine family with brothers and sisters in a home congregation serving each other's needs and at the same time reaching out to the lost.

1. Observations from Evangelicals. The organized local church is presently the subject of much attention by evangelicals whose denominational structure traditionally contrasts with the New Testament pattern.

The late Francis Schaeffer observed from his study of Matthew 18:15-17, "There is an indication here that there is some structure to which we may bring our brother when we have had a falling out – a structure which makes a distinction between those in that structure and those out of it."[63] Dr. Schaeffer continues to comment from Acts 16:1-5 on the structure of the churches that were established by Paul and Barnabas on their first missionary journey:

As the missionary journey progressed, once more individuals were brought to salvation, but they soon joined together in a specific, observable structure, an organization with form. Throughout Paul's missionary journey we see a stress on the formation of churches.[64]

After Schaeffer comments on the importance of the New Testament picture of individual local churches as a reality he says,

The picture is clear. As Paul moves over the Roman Empire, as other Christians move over the Roman Empire, individuals are saved and local congregations are organized. And this, I believe, is a pattern that holds for the church till Jesus comes.[65]

A final observation from Schaeffer is on local church polity:

The letters of Paul and the book of Acts indicate something of the specific form these congregations took. We know, for example, that the churches had offices. Acts 14:23 reads, "And when they had ordained [or appointed] them elders in every church, and had prayed with fasting, they commended them to the Lord, on whom they believed" ... there simply is no doubt of the fact that there were elders. The church did not sit there as a group of believers with no form ... Missionaries on missionary journeys produced not only individual Christians, but also churches with officers.[66]

Thiessen says,

In response to the preaching of Peter and the other apostles, 3,000 "received the word gladly," were baptized, and added unto them "that day" (Acts 2:14, 41). A little later this church had grown to 5,000 (Acts 4:4). It is clear that the believers acted as a corporate unit. They had a definite doctrinal standard (Acts 2:42); they had fellowship with one another as believers (*ibid*); they observed the ordinances of baptism and the Lord's Supper (vv. 42, 47); they met for public worship (v. 46); and they contributed to the support of the needy (v. 44, 45). Surely, we have here the marks of an organized local church, even if the organization was only loose as yet.[67]

Earl D. Radmacher introduces a chapter on "The Doctrine of the Local Church" saying,

> The working method of God in the world at any given time is to carry out His purpose through the members of the body of Christ who are living in the world at that time, and the New Testament always views these members of the body as banded together in groups known as local churches. Thus the church is in the world in the form of local churches ... The local church is God's agency in the world, transacting God's business ... That these local churches hold a place of prime importance in the mind of God and are the means through which God's program is to be accomplished can be clearly shown by a careful study of the New Testament revelation.[68]

What these evangelicals have observed concerning the structure of the church in the New Testament is outlined in the following.

2. Organized local churches seen throughout the New Testament. The picture of the work of the church in the New Testament goes beyond soul-winning to establishing and organizing new converts into local churches with leadership for spiritual growth and evangelistic direction.

a. Luke's history reveals the development and existence of local churches as distinct autonomous entities within the universal body of Christ that are organized with elders, teachers, deacons, and evangelists (Acts 6:1-6; 11:22, 26; 13:1; 14:23; 15:2, 4, 6, 22; 20:17).

b. The Philippian church was organized with overseers (bishops) and deacons (Phil. 1:1).

c. The Thessalonian church was organized under a plurality of leaders who were "over" the church and caringly worked in behalf of that local body of Christians (1 Thess. 5:12-15).

d. The churches of Crete. Paul charged Titus, who was at Crete, to set in order the things that were lacking and to appoint elders in every city where there was a local church (Titus 1:5). Local churches that have not developed the final level of leadership lack a full capability to give the kind of leadership direction and spiritual assistance needed by its members.

e. James speaks of calling for "the elders of the church" to pray for the sinful and the sick (James 5:14). This language takes both the local eldership and its purpose for granted and exhorts members to take advantage of the spiritual leadership God has provided the home congregation.

f. Peter says that local churches are "entrusted" to elderships as flocks of sheep are entrusted to shepherds (1 Peter 5: 1-3). The analogy of shepherds and flocks illustrates the care God has provided for his little lambs.

In summary, the local church in the New Testament was either fully organized according to the New Testament pattern or was expected to pursue full organizational development. This structure with evangelists, shepherds, teachers and deacons is divinely designed to serve the needs of God's precious people and to expedite the work assigned to the local church. For this reason God wants his people to take up spiritual residence in a local church. This is one reason why he exhorts us not to forsake "the assembling of ourselves together" (Heb. 10:25). Active membership in a local congregation is God's plan for the assistance and spiritual growth of every one of God's children.

B. The Local Church Is Organized to Work and Worship

1. Organized for evangelism.

a. Deacons selected in the Jerusalem church (Acts 6:1-7).

The deacons selected by the church in Jerusalem not only relieved their widows but also enabled the apostles to continue steadfastly in prayer and preaching. Organizing deacons into the local body allowed the preachers to continue to evangelize the lost so that "the word of God spread, and the number of disciples multiplied greatly in Jerusalem, and a great company of the priests were obedient to the faith."

b. The church at Syrian Antioch (Acts 11:19-26). Paul and Barnabas were assembled with this local church for an entire year "and taught a great many people." This evangelistic effort resulted in such a harvest of souls that Luke records "the disciples were called Christians first at Antioch." Later evangelistic efforts by this same church included separating Barnabas and Paul from their midst for a special evangelistic effort (Acts 13:1-4). Rather than expressing any regrets that this soul-winning team was to be separated from their midst to go elsewhere, this church seems to have been eager to send them out, as the Holy Spirit directed.

c. Local churches regularly supported Paul for evangelism (2 Cor. 11:8; Phil. 4:15-16). Behind organizing deacons to serve special needs in the local church, behind separating evangelists from the local membership for evangelism and sending them out, and behind collecting and sending wages to them for support, there has to be some sort of administrative organization at the local level. Whether or not a congregation has elders, the local church is to pursue its assigned work, its purpose for being a local church of Christ, which requires a cooperation that only an organized local membership can achieve and maintain.

2. Organized for edification. This Scripture speaks to a leadership that is conscientious towards leading every member into spiritual growth and ministry development.

a. Spiritual growth is essential for the preservation of every Christian (Eph. 4:11-16). Efforts by the local leadership to direct new Christians into spiritual growth must proceed immediately after conversion (Matt. 28:20; Heb. 5:12a; 1 Peter 2:2; 2 Peter 3:18). Growth in sound doctrine and faithful

Christian living is essential to keep Christ's newborn children from being "tossed to and fro and carried about with every wind of doctrine" (See also Heb. 5:12a; 1 Peter 2:1-2; 2 Peter 3:18; 1 John 2:26-27; 4:1-6; Jude 16-23). The growth of the Christian must be adequate to meet Satan in the work force, on the campus, in entertainment choices and at home. The Lord has organized the local church to lead every member into spiritual growth and maturity (Keep in mind Paul's urgent address to the eldership at Ephesus, Acts 20:18-31). The local church – organized and functioning as God designed it – should be viewed by every member as the center of Christian education and the Christian's own special support base.

b. Personal ministry to others expected of every Christian (Eph. 4:11-12). One of the divine purposes for organizing the local church with evangelists, shepherds and teachers is "for the equipping of the saints for the work of ministry." We must not view the "ministers" of a local church as confined to the leadership. All Christians are ministers and servants. The Lord has endowed all of us with special ministry abilities, gifts from God, to be used for the benefit of others. Not all gifts mentioned in the New Testament were miraculous,[69] and not all have the same gifts (1 Cor. 12:28-30; Eph. 4:7-11). Christ wants each of his servants to discover his or her peculiar gifts and develop them for ministry to others (Rom. 12:6-8; Eph. 4:12; 1 Peter 4:10). Since attendance at worship services is in itself inadequate to discover and develop our ministry gifts, the Lord has also gifted the local church with a leadership whose assignment includes equipping the members for their special ministries.

Is there not, then, a responsibility on the part of leadership to prepare themselves professionally to meet the needs of those entrusted to them? And is there not a responsibility of the membership to yield themselves from time to time to ministry training?

c. Expediting the edification process requires:

(1) Cooperation of all leadership personnel. While evangelists, shepherds and teachers have distinctive functions, they

are all assigned to the leadership role of building up the local membership (read again Eph. 4:11-16). A wise leadership will recognize its need for constant intercommunication with all those whose job descriptions overlap their own.

(2) Planning and implementing workable assignments. We must not be afraid of programs. A program is but a strategy of action. Without planning and implementing, how can a local membership engage unanimously in a particular activity? The program is but the design to expedite the work and worship of the church. Consider:

(a) Worship assemblies. The activities of the worship assembly are to be planned and implemented for the edification of the people (1 Cor. 14:26). Paul said the assembly is to be conducted in a fitting and orderly manner (1 Cor. 14:40). Could a local church worship together on the Lord's Day without planning and implementation? Nothing is to be second-rated by lack of planning or inadequate or unprepared ministers. God is to be praised and glorified, and the saints are to be edified. This requires planning, training, implementing, and prayer.

(b) Pulpit preaching. God has designed public preaching in the local church as one of the most effective means of building up the body of Christ (1 Tim. 4:6-16; 2 Tim. 4:1-4). Reproving and rebuking are effective when they are couched in longsuffering and Bible teaching. Strength of conviction and boldness of spirit in proclamation gain the attention, drive home the message, and secure the people in the faith. But this boldness is not to be equated with bombastic negativism and destructive criticism that produce despondency rather than edification. Mere speeches without biblical substance, reading sermons rather than proclaiming, and poor delivery because of inadequate preparation transform the assembly into boredom and triteness. God wants the message in the Word proclaimed that his people may be educated, edified and stabilized. Paul charged the preacher: "Preach the word ... do the work of an evangelist, fulfill your ministry" (2 Tim. 4:1-5).

(c) Systematic Bible study. Opportunities should exist for

Sunday Bible classes, midweek services, ladies' Bible classes, and more personalized home Bible studies fitted to individual and family needs. There should be Bible study programs for all age levels.

(d) Preparation and encouragement for evangelism. Preparation should include doctrinal instruction and training in methodology that has proven expedient and workable for implementing evangelism.

(e) Marriage counseling for single, married, and divorced members. This requires specialized training, experience, and spiritual maturity, in addition to Bible knowledge, whether for personal or group counseling.

(f) Leadership training for elders, teachers, deacons, preachers, and others who have assumed work assignments in the local church.

(g) Lectureships addressing current challenges. Doctrinal, practical, domestic, brotherhood problems affect the faith and stability of the local membership.

The list could go on. The point is that God has organized the local church with ministries to give guidance and assistance for the spiritual development of the local membership.

3. Organized for relief (Acts 6:1-6; 11:29-30; 1 Tim. 5:16). Read these Scriptures to see that some structure was necessarily inherent in the local churches to implement the relief of needy members. Consider from Romans 15:25-26; 1 Corinthians 16:1-4; 2 Corinthians 8:1-9:15; Philippians 4:10, 15-18 that some kind of local church structure was necessary to plan and coordinate a contribution within the churches and to see that it reached those in need.

4. Organized for discipline and restitution (1 Cor. 5:1-13). The church at Corinth was directed to assemble together in the name of the Lord to discipline the immoral brother. In this way the church expedited the instruction to "deliver such a one to Satan" and to "purge out the old leaven" of sin in their midst. It was not merely an individual matter of withdrawing personal fellowship. This is clearly an official action of the organized local church. Hopefully such organized and unified

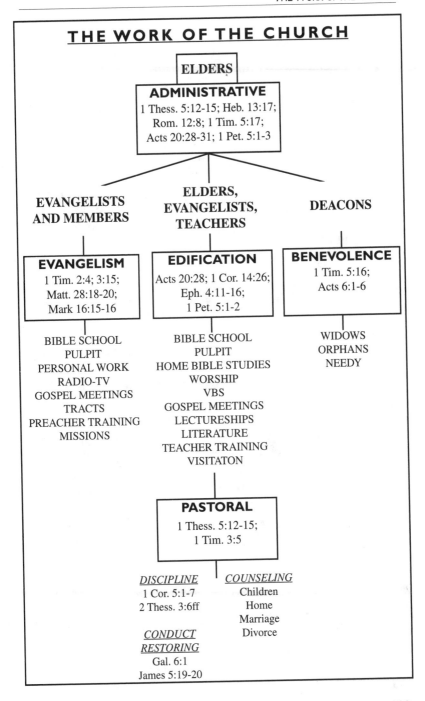

THE WORK OF THE CHURCH

ELDERS

ADMINISTRATIVE
1 Thess. 5:12-15; Heb. 13:17;
Rom. 12:8; 1 Tim. 5:17;
Acts 20:28-31; 1 Pet. 5:1-3

EVANGELISTS AND MEMBERS

ELDERS, EVANGELISTS, TEACHERS

DEACONS

EVANGELISM
1 Tim. 2:4; 3:15;
Matt. 28:18-20;
Mark 16:15-16

EDIFICATION
Acts 20:28; 1 Cor. 14:26;
Eph. 4:11-16;
1 Pet. 5:1-2

BENEVOLENCE
1 Tim. 5:16;
Acts 6:1-6

BIBLE SCHOOL
PULPIT
PERSONAL WORK
RADIO-TV
GOSPEL MEETINGS
TRACTS
PREACHER TRAINING
MISSIONS

BIBLE SCHOOL
PULPIT
HOME BIBLE STUDIES
WORSHIP
VBS
GOSPEL MEETINGS
LECTURESHIPS
LITERATURE
TEACHER TRAINING
VISITATON

WIDOWS
ORPHANS
NEEDY

PASTORAL
1 Thess. 5:12-15;
1 Tim. 3:5

DISCIPLINE
1 Cor. 5:1-7
2 Thess. 3:6ff

COUNSELING
Children
Home
Marriage
Divorce

CONDUCT RESTORING
Gal. 6:1
James 5:19-20

action would accomplish its desired impact upon the brother in bringing him to repentance and to restoration of fellowship with Christ and once again with the church.

The idea of local church discipline should not be viewed as confined to the severe measures of withdrawal of fellowship from damaged and sinful brethren. We do not want to shoot our wounded. Rather we must desire and implement healing where it is possible (Gal. 6:1-5). Discipline begins with preventative action, preferably by the leadership, with understanding, encouragement and whatever doctrinal and/or moral support is necessary (1 Thess. 5:12-15; Heb. 13:17) to achieve some spiritual stability so that the ultimate disciplinary action is avoided.

IV. Conclusion

The body of Christ in the first century, under direct administration of the apostles, followed a pattern to accomplish her mission. The universal body was structured into local churches and organized with preachers, teachers and deacons under the direction of elders. These local churches engaged in effective evangelism, edification, relief, worship and discipline and successfully financed all their work from local treasuries. Abuses and imperfections in membership and leadership are not valid reasons for indicting this New Testament plan as unworkable. The local church must struggle to attain the ideal as revealed in the word of God. In such a conscientious effort the church can attain a happy degree of mission accomplishment. The by-product will be peace, unity, spiritual growth and congregational stability.

Quick-Answer Questions

1. How do we glorify God in the local church?
2. What do you believe should be the prime motives for beginning a new local church?
3. Do you believe members are justified in seeking out and desiring a congregation that can provide quality preaching, leadership and edification? Explain.

4.   What obligations do you think local leadership has to its membership to provide the very best it can in work, worship and edification?

Discussion Questions

1.   How should the New Testament's teaching of the organized local church affect "floating" members?

2.   In light of Ephesians 4:11-16; 1 Thessalonians 5:12-15; and Hebrews 13:17, how should members of the universal church be expected to respond?

3.   If the program of education in the school system where your children attend were commensurate with the attention and quality of Christian education in the local church where you are a leader, would you be satisfied?

4.   What can be done, or what are you doing, to upgrade the quality and fruitfulness of the Christian education and edification in the local church where you are a member?

CHAPTER 11

THE IDENTITY AND ACCEPTABILITY OF WORSHIP

As far as mankind has been traced to his ancient past, expressions of his search for and his devotion to God have been found. Truly man has been created a compulsive worshiper. From the beginning God provided for that urge to be satisfied by revealing both the purpose of worship and the means by which that worship is to be offered to God. The purpose has never been arbitrary; it has always been to God's glory and the benefit of the worshiper. In each dispensation (Patriarchal, Mosaic, Christian) God has revealed the means by which worship is to be offered.

I. Worship Defined

Our word "worship" is nowhere defined in Scripture. It must be defined in part by the terms from which it is translated. There are a number of words in the Greek New Testament that can be translated "worship." We will confine this study to two words.

A. *Proskuneo*

This verb form, meaning "to make obeisance, do reverence to (from *pros,* towards, and *kuneo,* to kiss), is the most frequent word rendered to worship. It is used of an act of homage or reverence."[70]

It should be emphasized that *proskuneo* is a distinct act

of worship that is to be distinguished from a life of worship-ful service to Christ that generally characterizes Christians (for this definition see *latreuo* below). The worship (*proskuneo*) that is performed as a special act of reverence is illustrated in Abraham's statement to the young men that accompanied him to the sacrifice of Isaac: "Stay here with the donkey, the lad and I will go yonder and worship, and we will come back to you" (Gen. 22:5). The Septuagint[71] uses a form of *proskuneo*. It is clear that Abraham and Isaac went to a particular place to perform a special act of worship as God had directed. They worshiped, and after completing their worship they returned.

Hence all of life is not *proskuneo* worship. This is illus-trated again in John 9:38 where it is said of the blind man whom Jesus healed, "And he worshiped him." This constitut-ed an act of worship. Again, after seeing the risen Lord, Thomas was so impressed that he paid homage to Christ, saying, "My Lord and my God!" (John 20:28). In these instances, worship is a completed act that is distinguished from the rest of their service to God.

While worship is an act, it is not to be equated with play-acting, merely going through the motions of worship. It is no mechanically performed ritual. Rather it is spontaneous, from the heart, genuine.

B. *Latreuo*

This is a verb that means "to serve, to render religious service or homage."[72] Stephen uses the word to say, "God turned and gave them up to *serve* the host of heaven" (Acts 7:42). The result of Israel's idolatry was the immoral and per-verted lifestyle by which they served their gods.

Paul says, "But this I confess to you, that according to the Way which they call a sect, so I *worship* the God of my fa-thers" (Acts 24:14). Paul's "worship" in this verse (*latreuo*) refers to his way of life. This lifestyle service to Christ is what is meant when Paul said, "I beseech you therefore, brethren, by the mercies of God, that you present your bodies a living sacrifice, holy, acceptable to God, which is your reasonable *service*" (Rom. 12:1). The NASB renders it, "which is your spiritual *service of worship.*" Thus *latreuo* is the worshipful lifestyle that characterizes the Christian's daily walk

We should not think of worship as confined to praise or a worship activity in a church house. It can be a distinct act such as commemorating the Lord's death in observing the Lord's supper, which is *proskuneo,* or it can be our daily service to Christ by conscientiously keeping his commandments, which is *latreuo.*

C. Maintain the Distinction

Jesus used both terms when answering Satan's bid for worship: "Away with you, Satan! For it is written, 'You shall worship (*proskuneo*) the Lord your God, and him only you shall serve' (*latreuo*)" (Matt. 4:10). Both the acts of worship as commanded and authorized in God's Word and the life of daily service to God according to his Word are distinctive means of worship.

II. The Distinct Identity of Christian Worship

The Lord himself instructs us in what has always constituted acceptable and unacceptable worship (*proskuneo*):

> But the hour is coming, and now is, when the true worshipers will worship the Father in spirit and truth; for the Father is seeking such to worship him. God is Spirit, and those who worship him must worship in spirit and truth (John 4:23-24).

> Hypocrites! Well did Isaiah prophesy of you saying: These people draw near to me with their mouth. And honor me with their lips, But their heart is far from me. And in vain do they worship me, Teaching as doctrines the commandments of men (Matt. 15:7-9).

The hour that was coming, from Jesus' vantage point in time, is the Christian age. He distinguishes "the true worshipers" from the "hypocrites" by contrasting the worship that is "in spirit" to a pretense of worshipful devotion (*sebontai*)[73] that is not from the heart. He further distinguishes "the true worshipers," who worship in "truth" according to God's Word, from the hypocrites whose worship was according to the "the commandments of men."

A.   The Distinctive Elements by Which True Worship Is Identified

Jesus speaks of "true worshipers" and says that God can identify true worshipers: "The Father is seeking such to worship him." True worshipers necessitate a standard of true worship, and Jesus tells us the standard of true worship is "spirit and truth." These are the standard elements by which we identify true worship and by which God identifies true worshipers.

1. Spirit. "Spirit" expresses the character of worship; it is worship from a genuinely reverent and grateful heart. The "spirit" of true worshipers is the sincere *how* of true worship. This "spirit" or "heart" was lacking in the mere lip service of the hypocritical worshipers of Matthew 15:8.

2. Truth. The "truth" is the standard of true worship as revealed in God's Word. Jesus clarified this in his prayer for the apostles: "Sanctify them by your truth. Your word is truth" (John 17:17). This "truth" speaks of what we *do* in worship and, therefore, of what is authorized in worship. What "true worshipers" do to worship God must be authorized by his word. The word of God defines and authorizes the "truth" of true worship. Therefore, what God has authorized for worship can be distinctively identified.

This "truth" of God's Word is what was lacking in the "vain" worship of the hypocrites in Matthew 15:9. They worshiped according to the commandments of men rather than the truth authorized in God's Word.

In an attempt to keep the definition of the "truth" of worship from being limited to the word of God, the word "reality" has sometimes been substituted for the word "truth." However, not all reality is truth. John says, "No lie is of the truth" (1 John 2:21). A lie is reality, but it is neither the truth nor "of the truth" of God's Word by which we define true worship. Jesus said we come to "know the truth" by his word (John 8:32). The Holy Spirit identifies the light of God's Word as the truth in which we are to walk (1 John 1:5-7). He equates the truth that is in us with the word that is in us (1 John 2:4-5). He equates the truth with the word of the commandment (2 John 4). The reality of true worship is determined only by God's Word.

B. We *"Must* Worship in Spirit and Truth"

"Must" is absolute. Compare Jesus' statement, "You *must* be born anew" (John 3:3). Worship in spirit and truth is not an option: "God is spirit, and those who worship him *must* worship in spirit and truth." Acceptable worship "must" be from the heart and "must" be authorized by God's Word. This emphasizes the significance of offering only acceptable worship to God.

C. Acceptable Worship Can Be Identified

Jesus said that "the true worshipers will worship the Father in spirit and truth" and that "the Father is seeking *such* to worship him." Since God is seeking true worshipers to worship him, they obviously can be identified. Since true worshipers can be identified, it is also true that true worship can be identified. We can, therefore, identify the "spirit and truth" in God's Word that is essential to acceptable worship.

ACCEPTABLE WORSHIP	
God seeks such:	John 4:23, 24
True Worshipers	
(who) MUST worship in:	Identity of
1. Spirit – Character, Heart	True Worshipers
2. Truth – Standard, Authority,	and
God's Word.	True Worship

Christian worship has a distinctive identity. It is that worship set out in the pattern of sound words by which we "must worship" the Lord.

III. The Object of True Worship (Matt. 4:10; Rev. 19:10; 22:8-9)

The New Testament opens and closes with the same instruction to all: "Worship God." God is a Person with feelings who wants us to worship him from the heart. Thoughtless pretense in Sunday morning worship services – manifested by ho-hum inattentiveness and glassy-eyed stares testifying that the heart and mind are elsewhere – is without value to the worshiper and gains no points with God. It must be understood that our worshipful acts are to be prompted by our recognition of God's incomparable greatness and power and wisdom and from our deep gratitude for his redemptive love manifested in Christ and the cross.

The worship of such great spirits as Abraham, Job, David and Daniel are in marked contrast to the mere outward unfeeling rituals that characterized apostate Israel described in the prophets:

> To what purpose is the multitude of your sacrifices to me? says the Lord. I have had enough of burnt offerings of rams and the fat of fed cattle. I do not delight in the blood of bulls, or of lambs or goats.... Bring no more futile sacrifices... I cannot endure iniquity and the sacred meeting (Isa. 1:11-13).

> I hate, I despise your feast days, and I do not savor your sacred assemblies. Though you offer me burnt offerings and your grain offerings, I will not accept them, nor will I regard your fattened peace offerings.Take away from me the noise of your songs, for I will not hear the melody of your stringed instruments. But let justice roll down like water, and righteousness as a mighty stream (Amos 5:21-24).

Although Israel's worship could be observed at every turn, it was vain due to an unresponsive heart and disobedient lifestyle. Their worship was merely perfunctory, going through the motions. Today's worship by song, the observance of the

Lord's Supper and prayer are all vain if performed in no more than a ritualistic and unfeeling manner.

God is to be revered, honored, respected, loved and enjoyed. All of this is to be genuinely expressed in our worship of God.

IV. False Worship

This is the opposite of worship authorized by God's Word.

A. Vain Worship (Matt. 15:6-9; Mark 7:6-9)

As Christians, we died to all the religious teachings and regulations that are "according to the commandments and doctrines of men" (Col. 2:18-22). However sincere, our worship is "vain" if we worship according to the teachings of men.

B. Ignorant Worship (Acts 17:23)

Worship without the knowledge of the true God or without the knowledge of the truth by which we are to worship God is ignorant worship. Paul's language is appropriate here: "For I bear them witness that they have a zeal for God, but not according to knowledge" (Rom. 10:2).

C. Will Worship (Col. 2:18)

Will worship is "voluntary adopted worship, whether unbidden or forbidden, not that which is imposed by others, but which one affects."[74] This is also rendered "self imposed religion." It is worship one imposes upon himself as an access to God. It is worship that has no ground in Scripture; it is but the invention of the human mind. This can be identified in the religious subjectivism of our time that worships God according to what one feels that God will accept.

V. Conclusion

Worship has been designed by God and revealed in his Word. God is himself the only object of our worship. The how (spirit) and the what (truth) of worship revealed in the New Testament are sufficient to satisfy man's inner desire to express himself to God. True worship glorifies God as the true worshiper subjects his will to the Father's will. True Worship is beneficial to the worshiper because when he knows God's will for true worship and worships according to that will, he knows that his worship is acceptable. Worship that is acceptable to God can be identified in Scripture and distinguished from all worship that is unacceptable.

Quick-Answer Questions

1. State the difference between *proskuneo* worship and *katreuo*.
2. Is worship confined to a church service?
3. Can the worship the Lord speaks of in John 4:23-24 be identified? How?
4. Are there certain worship acts God wants us to offer? Be specific.
5. Who is the object of worship?
6. Define and illustrate will-worship.

Discussion Questions

1. If there is no Scriptural way to identify true worship, could we identify false worship? Elaborate.
2. Define and illustrate from Scripture how we can identify true worship.
3. Discuss the need for individual discipline as a requirement for worshiping in spirit.
4. Discuss how a departure from the pattern of true worship will produce vain worship. See Matthew 15:8-9.

CHAPTER 12

THE LORD'S SUPPER

The institution, significance, and time element of the Lord's supper will be taken into account in this lesson.

I. The Lord's Supper Instituted by Christ

Read each of the following accounts thoughtfully in preparation for the study (Matt. 26:17-30; Mark 14:12-26; Luke 22:7-20).

A. The Occasion

The Passover was a Jewish feast commemorating Israel's deliverance from Egyptian bondage. During this feast with his disciples Jesus instituted the Lord's Supper for the church to commemorate our deliverance from bondage to sin.

B. Something "New" for the Coming Kingdom

Both Matthew and Mark record the Lord's promise to the disciples to commune with them in the Lord's Supper. But, as Jesus said, it would be in "that day when I drink it *new* with you in my Father's kingdom" (Matt. 26:29; Mark 14:25). The significance of that *newness* comprehends the following:

1. The Lord's Supper to be observed in the new kingdom under a new covenant. Jesus said to the disciples that the fruit of the vine represented his blood which was shed for the new covenant and for the remission of sins (Matt. 26:28). Then he said he would commune with them in the fruit of the vine in the new kingdom (Matt. 26:29). At his death Christ abolished the old Jewish economy (Eph. 2:15) and consecrated a new covenant — "the new and living way" — for his new kingdom reign (Matt. 26:28; Heb. 10:19-20). Paul then connects the Corinthians' participation in the Lord's Supper to communion with Christ (1 Cor. 10:16) under the new covenant (1 Cor. 11:25). Hence, the new kingdom – the reign of Christ – had arrived at Corinth with a new memorial for a new covenant people. In the Lord's Supper Christ is fulfilling his promise to commune with his disciples in the new kingdom.

2. The Lord's Supper to commemorate a new deliverance. Jesus is our Passover (1 Cor. 5:7) who by means of his cross delivers us from the bondage of sin and death. He now passes over our sins by accounting our faith in him for righteousness. Remembering Christ in the Lord's Supper is the Christian's expression of faith that his death was the means of our deliverance from bondage to sin. It is a time of celebration for grateful Christians.

3. The Lord's Supper to be observed on a new day. The Israelites kept the Sabbath, the last day of the week, as a reminder that they were delivered from bondage (Deut. 5:12-15). On Sunday, the first day of the week, Christians remember our deliverance in the Lord's Supper. Christ's resurrection on Sunday is the confirmation of his victory over death at the cross, and we proclaim his victory over death on the day of his resurrection (1 Cor. 11:26). Therefore, the Christian's confidence that he was raised on the first day of the week inspires us on that day to proclaim his death as the moment of our victory from bondage to sin.

The new kingdom-reign of Christ, the new Covenant, the new deliverance of his new people and the new memorial to the Deliverer are so interrelated with the King and his new covenant people that they cannot be separated.

II. The Significance of the Lord's Supper

The Lord's Supper is not a mere ritual without beneficial significance. It is related to the redemptive work of Christ on the Cross, to the fellowship and unity of the local church, and to the holiness of the body of Christ as the people set apart unto God.

A.   It Is a Communion (1 Cor. 10:15-22)

From *koinonia*, translated here *communion*, elsewhere by *fellowship, participation, sharing*, it is "a having in common, partnership, fellowship, denotes the share which one has in anything, a participation, fellowship recognized and enjoyed … of sharing in the realization of the effects of the Blood (i.e., the Death) of Christ and the Body of Christ, as set forth by the emblems in the Lord's Supper, 1 Cor. 10:16."[75]

Eating the Lord's Supper expresses the fellowship we have with Christ because of his atoning work at the cross and the fellowship we have with each other as members of his one body (see 1 Cor. 10:16-17).

B.   It Is a Commemoration, a Proclamation, and a Time for a Self-examination

1. A commemoration, that is, a memorial (1 Cor. 11:26-33), "Do this in remembrance of me." What Christians remember in the Lord's Supper is the person and work of Christ in delivering us from sin and death. Of course, that is the Christian's waking thought. But this remembrance is a special memorial to Christ at a special time and in a special way for the glory of Christ and the benefit of his special people.

2. A proclamation (1 Cor. 11:26), from *katangello,* an evangel, related to *evangelist.* The Lord's Supper is a silent proclamation, a heralding or preaching, of the death of Christ as his victory over death for the sins of the world.

3. A time for a self-examination (1 Cor. 11:28-32). The Christian is to "examine himself" at the time of the Lord's Supper with a view toward "discerning the Lord's body." "Discerning the Lord's body" may refer to gratefully remembering Christ on the cross. It seems to me in light of the language of verse 31, where the body of Christ is clearly the church, that it means the Corinthian Christians were to examine themselves to see if they contributed to the division or the unity of the body with a view toward correcting any mis-conduct (this is the context to which Paul addresses himself). For Paul made it clear that such division in the church at Corinth made it impossible to eat the Lord's Supper (1 Cor. 11:18-20). Also participation in idolatry, or any form of pa-ganism or worldliness, also makes it impossible to eat the Lord's Supper. Paul says, "I do not want you to have fellow-ship with demons. You *cannot* drink the cup of the Lord and the cup of demons; you *cannot* partake of the Lord's table and the table of demons" (1 Cor. 10:14-21). One may ingest un-leavened bread and fruit of the vine without eating the Lord's Supper, without communion with Christ.

Understanding the significance and purpose of the Lord's Supper will do much to explain why the Lord wants his peo-ple to observe the Lord's Supper on a regular weekly basis. If all the body of Christ each Lord's Day examined themselves as we are taught, we would have to see a more loving, caring, sensitive and unified church in just a few weeks. Surely we would see the difference such a sincere introspection would produce in a few months. Without a doubt we would see a wondrous transition of conduct toward each other and toward the world in a year! After 52 serious, thoughtful examinations according to the guidelines of the new covenant we would have to see some marked differences in the local body. Think of the beautiful outcome of unity and purity and sensitivity toward one another in the local church after five or 10 years of sin-cere self-examinations while eating the Lord's Supper!

The Lord's Supper is not only to remember Christ's death on the cross but also to remember that we are to die to our-selves, to be motivated to live righteous lives and to live for the unity of the body.

III. The Time Element for Observing the Lord's Supper

Paul instructed the church at Corinth in the Lord's Supper. The same instruction was given by all the apostles to all the churches (1 Cor. 4:17; 7:17; 14:37; 2 Thess. 2:15). The Lord's

Supper was to be observed "often" (1 Cor. 11:26). How often is the question.

A. Regularly and Frequently

The Corinthian church was abusing the Lord's Supper. Paul corrects them by reminding them of his original instruction (1 Cor. 11:23). It is important to see the seriousness of his instruction, that he couches it between two statements of instructions or directives (1 Cor. 11:17, 34). After concluding his instructions, he says, "And the rest will I set in order when I come." There is an order in Paul's instructions about the Lord's Supper that includes a regular and frequent coming together.

1. Upon the first day of every week. Paul's language makes it very clear that the Corinthian church had been directed to come together regularly to eat the Lord's Supper (1 Cor. 11:17, 18, 20, 33, 34). Read those scripture references. He is not teaching them anything new in these directives; instead, he is reminding them of what he had originally taught them when he first came to Corinth. Clearly before Paul wrote the Corinthian letter, he had earlier taught "the whole church" to come together regularly for the purposes of worship (1 Cor. 14:23-25) and of edification (1 Cor. 14:26). Thus, the pattern of apostolic teaching for all the churches was to come together regularly to be edified, to worship the Lord and to eat the Lord's Supper.

Then Paul gives another order (directive) to the Corinthians to lay aside some money for a benevolent purpose and directed them to do so "on the first day of every week" (1 Cor. 16:1-3). Why on the first day of *every* week? Because they were already coming together regularly on the first day of every week to be edified, to worship and to eat the Lord's Supper.

The writer of Hebrews exhorts brethren not to forsake "the assembling of ourselves together" (Heb. 10:25), leaving the distinct impression that there was a regular assembling of the saints and that they knew when and where it was.

2. Often. When Paul said, "For as often as you eat this

bread and drink this cup, you proclaim the Lord's death till he comes" (1 Cor. 11:26), he and the Corinthian church understood that it was as often as the first day of every week, as Paul had originally taught them.

When this instruction on the time element is coupled with the purpose of the Lord's Supper the reason for its frequency is both understood and deeply appreciated.

B. The Lord's Supper at Troas on the First Day of the Week (Acts 20:7-11)

Luke says that Paul and his traveling companions were gathered together on the first day of the week to break bread with the church at Troas. Apparently Paul and his company arrived too late on the prior Lord's Day to assemble with the church, for Luke says that after arriving at Troas, they stayed seven days before meeting with the saints on the first day of the week (Acts 20:6-7). The question is why they waited another seven days before assembling with the Troasian brethren. And how did they know that those brethren would assemble on the first day of the next week? It appears that it was taken for granted that the church at Troas would assemble to worship God, to be edified and to eat the Lord's Supper on the first day of every week. The statement of their purpose for gathering on the first day of week, "to break bread," is a clear implication that even if they had contact with the brethren in the middle of the week, they did not come together for that purpose prior to the Lord's Day.

Was it not common knowledge among the early churches that what was taught in one church by the apostles was taught in every church (1 Cor. 4:17; 2 Tim. 1:13)? The practice of the church at Troas in coming together on the first day of the week to break bread was commensurate with the instruction given by the apostles to the churches (2 Thess. 2:15).

C. Observe the Lord's Supper only on the First Day of the Week

We are reminded that Jesus said we are to worship the Lord in spirit and truth, the truth as taught in his Word. All worship must be authorized by God's Word. There is no authority to observe the Lord's Supper on any day other than the first day of the week.

But one may suggest that Jesus and the disciples ate the Lord's Supper on Thursday evening. However, we would also suggest that Jesus said the Lord's Supper would be observed for a new and different purpose, in a new and different kingdom, under a new and different covenant, and that the Holy Spirit makes it clear that all the churches of the New Testament observed the Lord's Supper on a new and different day from Thursday. We do not have new covenant authority to observe the Lord's Supper at any other time than on the first day of the week. We know that we are pleasing to God to observe the Supper only on the Lord's Day.

IV. Distinction Between the Lord's Supper and a Common Meal

While Jesus instituted the Lord's Supper during the Passover and while the early church may have eaten the Lord's Supper during or after a "love feast," the Lord's Supper itself was never intended to be a common meal.

A. Paul Distinguishes Between the Lord's Supper and a Common Meal

Paul's statement, "Therefore, my brethren, when you come together to eat" (1 Cor. 11:33), in context refers to eating the Lord's Supper. His follow-up statement, "But if anyone is hungry, let him eat at home" (1 Cor. 11:34), makes a clear distinction between the Lord's Supper and a common meal at home to satisfy one's hunger.

B. Luke Distinguishes Between the Lord's Supper and a Common Meal in Acts 2:42 And 2:46

1. The early church "continued steadfastly in the apostles' doctrine and fellowship, in the breaking of [the] bread and the prayers" (Acts 2:42). The definite article appears here in the original text before the word "bread," seeming to indicate a particular bread, the bread of the Lord's Supper. This breaking of the bread is observed in the context of the apostles' doctrine and the prayers, a worship context.

2. The "breaking bread" in Acts 2:46 is "at home," or "from house to house." It is the food of a common meal: "they ate their food with gladness and simplicity of heart."

SCRIPTURE REFERENCE	STATEMENT	TIME	PURPOSE
Acts 20:7	"gathered together"	"the first day of the week"	"to break bread"
1 Cor. 11:17	"come together"		
1 Cor. 11:18	"come together in the church"		
1 Cor. 11:20	"assemble yourselves together"		"to eat the Lord's Supper"
1 Cor. 11:33,34	"when ye come together" "your coming together"		"to eat"
1 Cor. 14:26	"ye come together"		"unto edifying"
Heb. 10:25	"not forsaking your own assembling together"		

C. Luke Distinguishes Between the Lord's Supper and a Common Meal in Acts 20:7 and 20:11

Luke says that on the first day of the week, "the *disciples* came together to break bread" and that Paul intended to depart on the morrow, which, of course, was the next day. Paul preached, and past midnight a young man asleep in a window fell out and was killed. Paul promptly raised him back to life. Then Luke records that "when *he* had come up, had broken bread and eaten, and talked a long while, even till daybreak, *he* departed" (Acts 20:11). There is a distinction in number between the "disciples," plural, in verse 7 who had gathered to break bread, and the "he," singular, Paul, who "had broken bread" in verse 11. This presents a distinction between the

Lord's Supper of verse 7 and the common meal that only Paul partook of in verse 11.

The Living Bible has verse 11 say the entire church ate the Lord's Supper on Monday morning after the raising of the young boy from the dead.[76] But, the disciples had gathered on the first day of the week to break bread, and Paul ate his breakfast on the morrow, the day *after* they had gathered to partake of the Lord's Supper. No acceptable exposition can equate verse 11 with the Lord's Supper.

V.   The Elements Used in the Lord's Supper

Unleavened bread and the fruit of the vine are the only elements authorized for the Lord's Supper.

A.   The Bread of the Passover Used by Jesus

Deuteronomy 16:1-8 required only unleavened bread in the house of those eating the Passover. Since the Lord instituted the Lord's Supper during the Passover feast, the bread he used was unleavened.

B.   The Fruit of the Vine Used by Jesus

Jesus referred to the cup he gave to the disciples as "this fruit of the vine" (Matt. 26:29). As the bread represents Christ's body, the fruit of the vine represents his shed blood for the forgiveness of our sins (Matt. 26:28). It does not matter whether it is fermented or straight from the squeezing if it is the fruit of the vine. There is no authorization for apple juice or Coca-Cola either as a replacement or an addition to the Lord's Supper.

VI. Conclusion

The Lord's Supper is worship designed for God's glory and for our own spiritual growth and development. It deserves our best efforts in concentration and sincere devotion. Each Christian should realize its significance and observe it in a manner worthy of the great love Christ manifested at Calvary.

Quick-Answer Questions

1.   What is the threefold purpose of the Lord's Supper?
2.   What did Paul mean when he said that we cannot par-
      take of the table of the Lord and the table of demons (1
      Cor. 10:21)?

Discussion Questions

1.   Paul says that Christ is our Passover (1 Cor. 5:7). Explain
      what that means. Then explain the connection between
      the cross of Christ and our observance of the Lord's
      Supper.
2.   Paul says the Christian's victory over death is Christ's
      cross (1 Cor. 15:56-57). What heartfelt response should
      accompany the Christian at the Lord's Supper as he re-
      members the death of Christ?
4.   Analyze the examination that is to take place in Christians
      as they observe the Lord's Supper. Does 1 Corinthians
      11:25 provide a divine criterion for that examination?
5.   Why were the Corinthians not able to eat the Lord's
      Supper even though they partook of the emblems (1 Cor.
      11:20)?
6.   Explain from 1 Corinthians how we know that Paul taught
      the church there to observe the Lord's Supper on the first
      day of every week.
7.   Is there biblical authority for observing the Lord's Supper
      at a time other than the first day of the week?
8.   Explain how the purpose of the Lord's Supper and ob-
      serving it on the first day of every week should produce
      stronger, more mature Christians.

CHAPTER 13

CHURCH MUSIC

God has instructed his people under both Old and New Covenants in the kind of music that glorifies him and benefits those who worship.

I. Worship Under the Old Covenant Included Instruments of Music

Under the Mosaic covenant the music conducted was both in song and with instruments. Special assignments were made by God through his prophets and overseen by King David (1 Chron. 25:1-7; 2 Chron. 29:25-30). It should be kept in mind that under the old covenant singers from the tribe of Levi and instruments of music were not merely authorized; they were commanded to be used at certain times to the glory of God.

After the return from Babylonian captivity, the ordinances for the restored temple services included singers and Levites to play the instruments (Neh. 12:1-47). Nehemiah says that Ezra the scribe was before them "with the musical instruments of David the man of God" and that the chiefs of the Levites were "to praise and give thanks, according to the command-ment of David the man of God" (Neh. 12:36, 24).[77]

The phrase, "man of God," is used in the Old Testament only of a prophet. Nehemiah shows the authorization for the singers and the musical instruments by referring to David as the man of God through whom the commandment came and by referring to Ezra who taught according to the law of Moses.

Keep in mind that the Mosaic covenant with its sacrificial system and worship requirements was abolished at the cross (Eph. 2:15). The covenant and its requirements were "changed" (Heb. 7:11-12). We must now look to the new covenant for the kind of music God has authorized for worship in his church.

II. Music in Worship Under the New Covenant Is Limited to Singing

The first historical reference we have under the new covenant of musical worship to God is of Paul and Silas singing in prison (Acts 16:25). Prophecy spoke of singing the salvation of God for the Gentiles (Rom. 15:9, which is a quotation from either 2 Sam. 22:50 or Ps. 18:49). We are instructed to sing with the spirit and with the understanding (1 Cor. 14:15). The types of songs designated for Christian worship are psalms, hymns and spiritual songs (Eph. 5:19; Col. 3:16). Melody, or music (NIV), is to be made in the heart while singing to the Lord and to one another. The heart is the instrument the Holy Spirit designated to accompany the singing. Through these Christian songs of worship, we also teach and admonish one another. The writer of Hebrews exhorts us, "Therefore by him let us continually offer sacrifice of praise to God, that is, the fruit of lips, giving thanks to his name" (Heb. 13:15). The fruit of lips includes singing. It is a sacrifice to God (Heb. 13:15). When we are made cheerful through God's good providence, we are to sing praise to God (James 5:13).

Here are the kinds of songs, the how of singing, the object of singing, and the purpose of singing. Instruments of music to accompany the worship of God in song are not found anywhere in the New Testament. We can do all that God wants us to do in the way of church music without an instrument; we can give God all the glory he is to receive from musical worship without an instrument, and we can receive all the benefit God has designed for us to receive in musical worship without an instrument.

III. Instruments of Music Not Authorized by the New Testament for Christian Worship

Christians are to do all in the name of Christ, that is, by his authority (Col. 3:17). There is no command authorizing the use of instruments in Christian worship, and there is no example of their use in Christian worship found in the New Testament. To use instruments of music in Christian worship is to do so without divine authorization.

IV. The Law of Exclusion

A fundamental teaching in the Old and New Testaments makes it incumbent upon those who would worship God acceptably to respect the silence of God's Word. This fundamental principle asks us to respect both the authority and the sufficiency of a commandment of God by neither adding to nor taking away from the thing commanded.

A. The Fundamental Principle

The following scriptures from both testaments lay out the principle in the clearest of terms:

> You shall not add to the word which I command you, nor take anything from it, that you may keep the commandments of the Lord your God which I command you (Deut. 4:2).

> Whatever I command you, be careful to observe it; you shall not add to it nor take away from it (Deut. 12:32).

> Do not add to his words, lest he reprove you, and you be found a liar (Prov. 30:6).

> Now these things, brethren, I have figuratively transferred to myself and Apollos for your sakes, that you may learn in us not to think beyond what is written, that none of you may be puffed up on behalf of one against the other (1 Cor. 4:6).

> For I testify to everyone who hears the words of the prophecy of this book: If anyone adds to these things, God will add to him the plagues that are written in this book; and if anyone takes away from the words of the book of this prophecy, God shall take away his part from the book of life, from the holy city, and from the things which are written in this book (Rev. 22:18-19).

One can hardly dispute the clarity of the language. Respect for the authority of that instruction must conclude that whatever is not commanded or is not by some statement authorized by God's Word is necessarily excluded as acceptable to God.

B. Illustrations of the Law of Exclusion

1. The "profane" offering of Nadab and Abihu (Lev. 10:1-2).

> Then Nadab and Abihu, the sons of Aaron, each took his censer and put fire in it, put incense on it, and offered profane fire before the Lord, which he had not commanded them. So fire went out from the Lord and devoured them, and they died before the Lord.

The NIV renders, "They offered unauthorized fire before the Lord, contrary to his command." God did not have to say explicitly that they were not to offer another kind of fire. His command to do a certain thing authorized only the thing commanded and, therefore, implicitly excluded any other kind of offering. Anything offered to God other than what he authorizes is "profane" and "contrary" to his word.

2. The prophet Balaam understood the law of exclusion (Num. 22:18).

> Then Balaam answered and said to the servants of Balak, 'Though Balak were to give me his house full of silver and gold, I could not go beyond the word of the Lord my God, to do less or more.'

The prophet had authority to speak the message God put into his mouth, no less and no more. All else is excluded.

3. The Holy Spirit reasons from the law of exclusion that Jesus could not have been a priest nor offered the gifts according to the law of Moses.

> Therefore, if perfection were through the Levitical priesthood (for under it the people received the law) what further need was there that another priest should arise according to the order of Melchizedek, and not be called after the order of Aaron? For the priesthood being changed, of necessity there is also a change of the law. For he of whom these things are spoken belongs to another tribe, from which no man has officiated at the altar. For it is evident that our Lord arose from Judah, of which tribe Moses spoke nothing concerning priesthood (Heb. 7:11-14).

When God gave instructions to takes priests from the tribe of Levi, he did not have to say explicitly that priests could not be taken from other tribes. But according to the law of exclusion, God's command to take priests from the tribe of Levi necessarily implied the exclusion of priests from any other tribe. The Holy Spirit reasons from this ground that since Jesus was of the tribe of Judah, he could not serve in the priesthood unless the law was changed that would allow priests from tribes other than Levi.

The Holy Spirit further reasons from the principle of exclusion that even Jesus could not offer the gifts if he were on earth since "there are priests who offer the gifts according to the law" (Heb. 8:4). According to the law priests were chosen from the tribe of Levi to offer the sacrifices. Since Jesus was of the tribe of Judah, he was necessarily excluded from offering the gifts according to the law of Moses.

C. Applications of the Law of Exclusion to Each Dispensation

1. The patriarchal dispensation (Gen. 6:13-14). God commanded Noah to build an ark. Had the Lord stopped his instruction there, Noah could have availed himself of whatever materials he judged adequate for the ark's construction. The command to build an ark necessarily excluded any other means of life support during the flood, but the construction material would have been left to Noah's judgment. However, God said, "Make yourself an ark *of gopher wood*" (Gen. 6:14). When God specified gopher wood as the building material, all other materials for the ark's construction were unauthorized and therefore excluded.

2. The Mosaic dispensation.

a. Nadab and Abihu (Lev. 10:1-2) as illustrated above.

b. The city where Israel was to offer sacrifices (Deut. 12:8-13). God's command to Israel was that after they inherited the land of promise, they were not to do according to their practice at that time, "every man doing whatever is right in his own eyes." They were to offer their sacrifices only in the city where he would put his name.

> [T]here will be the place where the Lord your God chooses to make his name abide. There you shall bring all that I command you: your burnt offerings, your sacrifices, your tithes ... Take heed to yourself that you do not offer your burnt offerings in every place that you see, but in the place which the Lord chooses, in one of your tribes, there you shall offer your burnt offerings, and there you shall do all that I command you.

God did not have to exclude by name all the other cities in Canaan as places where they were not to bring their sacrifices. His selection of the city where he would put his Name would exclude all other locations.

3. The Christian dispensation.

a. The elements used in the Lord's Supper are unleavened bread and the fruit of the vine. These are specified. Only these are authorized.

But one may object that the Bible does not say we cannot use tea in addition to these elements or apple juice in place of the fruit of the vine. But according to the law of exclusion, the Lord's selection and authorization of the bread and the fruit of the vine exclude all other elements in observing the Lord's Supper.

b. Singing is the only authorized music for Christian worship (Eph. 5:19; Col. 3:16; James 5:13). Music is a generic term: there are both vocal music and instrumental music. "Singing" is specified music. One can play an instrument without singing, and he can sing without playing. God has authorized only singing in the New Testament. No other kind of music is authorized, including instruments of music in Christian worship.

While the New Testament does not say we cannot use instruments of music in worship, it does tell us to "learn not to go beyond the things which are written" (1 Cor. 4:6 ASV). What God has specified and authorized – singing and making melody (music) in our hearts (Eph. 5:19) – excludes all other kinds of music.

V. Conclusion

A characteristic of the church of Christ is the distinctive nature of her worship. She offers her worship sacrifices from the heart – in spirit – and worships by the authorized truth of God's Word. Singing is specified for Christian music. All can agree that God will receive all the glory that he intends us to give him by singing without an instrument. The church can receive all the spiritual edification God wants us to receive by singing without an instrument, and we can make all the melody God wants us to make in the heart as the designated instrument to accompany our songs. When Christians sing from the heart, it gives glory to God and it edifies the church. Let us make a joyful noise to the Lord and sing with grace in our hearts to God.

Quick-Answer Questions

1. Does acceptable worship have to be authorized? See John 4:23-24.
2. Are instruments of music in worship authorized under the new covenant?
3. Can we sing songs without playing instruments? Can we play instruments without singing songs? Which do Ephesians 5:19 and Colossians 3:16 say?
4. Can we worship acceptably in song without a musical instrument?

Discussion Questions

1. In this lesson we have studied the law of exclusion. Do you believe the Scriptures teach that when God commands a certain thing to be done, all else is excluded? If not, how would you explain Deuteronomy 12:32 and 1 Corinthians 4:6?
2. What is the "strange fire which God had not commanded" (or "unauthorized fire contrary to God's command") of Leviticus 10:1-3? Is this a principle for us today?
3. Read Leviticus 10:3 and determine from the context of verses 1 and 2 how we sanctify the Lord
4. By whose authority would one use an instrument of music in worship today?
5. Do you believe Christians can worship God in song without an instrument and give to God all the glory and praise he intends and that we can receive all the benefit God intended? Explain.

SUPPLEMENTARY OUTLINE STUDIES

by Homer Hailey

Used by permission of Homer Hailey from his book, *Let's Go Fishing For Men*. Abilene, TX: Chronicle Publishing Co., 1951.

THE TWO COVENANTS
Hebrews 8

Failure of Bible teachers and students to make a proper division of the word of God, making no distinction between the Old and the New Covenants, has contributed to the existing confusion as to God's plan of salvation. Judaism, one of the greatest hindrances to Christianity through the centuries, is a consequence of this failure. Much of present-day denominational error is traceable to this failure to rightly divide the word of truth.

In this lesson we propose to study the relationship of both covenants to God's people in two dispensations, the purpose and passing of the first and the establishment of the second.

Definition of covenant:"An agreement by two or more parties to do or refrain from doing some act" The Old Covenant was an agreement between God and a nation; the New Covenant is an agreement between God and individuals. In both, blessings are promised and conditions stipulated. A covenant may be unconditional as between God and Abraham, Gen. 15:12-18, or conditional, as between God and Israel, Ex. 19:5, 6.

I.   THE OLD COVENANT

1. The Covenant was made between God and Israel, when the latter were brought out of Egypt to Mt. Sinai, Ex. 19:1-5: 24:1-8.

2. The law was a national law, given only to Israel, to govern them as a nation. Ex. 20:1, 2; 31:12-17; 34:27, 28; Deut. 5:1-6. It included no other peoples.

3. Not only was it a law given to a particular people, but it was given for a definite time, "Till the seed should come," Gal. 3:19, which was Christ, v. 16.

4. When speaking of the "law," how much do New Testament writers include in the term? *Genesis,* Gal. 4:21; (Gen. 16:15); *Exodus,* Rom 7:7 (Ex. 20:17); *Leviticus, Deuteronomy,* Matt. 22:35-39 (Lev. 19:18; Deut. 6:5); *Numbers,* Matt. 12:5 (Num. 28:9, 10); *Psalms,* John 10:34 (Ps. 82:6); *Prophets,* 1 Cor. 14:21 (Is. 28:11).

5. When shown from the Bible that the law was fulfilled and taken out of the way, then none of it can be appealed to as the law of a covenant under which people live today.

II. THE TEN COMMANDMENTS OF THE COVENANT

1. Those who would keep the Sabbath today make a distinction between "moral" and "ceremonial" parts of the law, a distinction which God does not make. They contend that the Ten Commandments were no part of that which was removed.

2. The Lord speaks of the Ten Commandments as "the covenant," Ex. 34:27, 28; Deut. 4:13; 9:9-11; 1 Kings 8:9, 21.

3. Therefore, if one can show that the covenant was fulfilled, removed and another made by Jehovah, he has shown that the Ten Commandments is not now the covenant under which the Christian lives.

III. THE PASSING OF THE OLD COVENANT

1. About midway between the beginning of the old and the beginning of the new, God declared He would made a "new covenant," Jer. 31:31-34. It should be "new," "different," "of the spirit," under which "all should know Him," with "sins remembered no more."

2. Jesus came to fulfill the first, Matt. 5:17, 18, which He declared He had done, John 19:28-30.

3. The Holy Spirit later declared the flrst had been fulfilled and taken out of the way, Eph. 2:14-16, with the new now in force, Heb. 8:6; 9:15;10:9,10; Matt. 26:28; Heb. 13:20. The second could not have been established until the first was removed, Heb. 7:12; 9:15-17.

4. The apostle Paul further testifies that we are not now under the old law: Not under the law, Rom. 6:15; dead to the law, Rom. 7:4; discharged from the law, Rom. 7:6; which law contained the "ten commandments," Rom 7:7.

5. This law, in its entirety, the one written on stones and all the rest, was done away in Christ, 2 Cor. 3:6-17.

IV. THE NEW COVENANT—THE GOSPEL OF CHRIST

1. All authority is now Christ's, Matt. 28:18-20.

2. All nations are included in the new covenant, Mark 16:15, 16; Luke 24:44-47.

3. The New Covenant is the fulfillment of the promise made to Abraham, Gal. 3:6-29. Under it, in Christ, all are "new creatures,"2 Cor. 5:17.

V. CONCLUSION

It is in the New, not the Old, that the sinner today finds his way to God, the terms of pardon, the conditions of fellowship with the Father and of eternal life. And it is in it that he finds the promises of God, which promises are guaranteed by the blood of God's own Son.

THE NEW TESTAMENT
AND
THE GREAT COMMISSION

The New Covenant is the covenant in Christ's blood, Matt. 26:28; Heb. 13:20; the covenant of the gospel of Christ, Mark 16:15, 16; Heb. 10:9, 10.

The word gospel means "good news" or "glad tidings." There were two commissions given by Jesus, one during His personal ministry, the other after His resurrection. Each contains its special theme of "good news" or gospel. To the Jew, it was good news that the kingdom was at hand. To the Gentile and Jew, after His resurrection, it was good news that Christ had died for sins and had been raised to rule over the kingdom. In this lesson we propose to consider the two commissions and the gospel of each.

I.   THE FIRST COMMISSION AND ITS GOSPEL

1. John the Baptist came preaching that the kingdom was "at hand," Matt. 3:1, 2. He was a forerunner of Jesus, Mal. 4:4-6; who bore witness of Him, Luke 1:16, 17; John 1:6-8; Luke 3:3-6.

2. Jesus—after John was delivered up—began preaching. His message also was the approaching nearness of the kingdom, Mark 1:14, 15; Matt. 4:17; 23.

3. The Twelve. Later in His ministry, Jesus selected the twelve whom he sent to the Jews only with the same message—

the approaching nearness of the kingdom, Matt. 10:5-7. To distinguish it from the commission given after His resurrection, this is often called "the limited commission"

4. The Seventy. After this He selected and sent forth seventy others, with the same message, likewise to Jews only, Luke 10:9.

5. Summary: The limited commission was given to the disciples before His death, sending them to the house of Israel, with the message of the approaching nearness of the kingdom, calling upon them to repent in preparation for its appearance.

II. THE GREAT COMMISSION, AND ITS GOSPEL

1. The promise to Abraham had included all nations; the first, or limited, commission included only Israel after the flesh. The commission after His resurrection, like the promise, included all families of the earth.

2. Matthew 28:18-20.

    (1) All authority now belongs to Christ.

    (2) Teach all nations: all to be taught, Jer. 31:33, 34; John 6:44, 45; Rom. 10:17.

    (3) Baptizing them into the name of the Father, Son, Holy Spirit. This is what they were to do, not necessarily to say. Each time they baptized "in the name of Christ," e.g., Acts 2:38, etc., this is what was done. (4) Teach to observe all—I have commanded you. Teaching follows, but only to teach as binding the things taught by Christ and the apostles.

3. Mark 16:15, 16

    (1) Preach the gospel—good news—not of the kingdom's nearness, but of Christ's death for our sins, His burial and resurrection, 1 Cor. 15:1-4.

    (2) Whole creation, all nations, fulfilling Gen. 12:3; 22: 18, etc.

    (3) Belief and baptism. Believe that which was preached, the gospel, Rom. 10:17; baptized, a

burial and resurrection, Rom. 6:3-5; Col. 2:12.

(4) Saved—equivalent to forgiveness of sins, Luke 24:47.

4. Luke 24:44-49.

(1) Christ fulfilled the promise and hope of the law and the prophets.

(2) His suffering (death) and resurrection for sins is the gospel.

(3) Repentance, remission of sins, in Christ's name, by His authority.

(4) Jerusalem, the place of beginning, Isa. 2:2, 3.

(5) Power, the Holy Spirit. They could not begin until it came, Acts 1:6-8.

5. Summary: Preach or teach—gospel (death, burial and resurrection of Jesus)—all nations—Jerusalem—power—believe—repentance—baptism—name—remission of sins—saved.

6. Acts 2 fulfills this every point: Preached—the gospel (death, burial and resurrection of Jesus)—all nations represented—Jerusalem—power (Holy Spirit)—believed (pricked in heart)—repentance—baptism—name—remission of sins.

III. THE THIEF ON THE CROSS—CAN HE BE APPEALED TO AS AN EXCEPTION?

1. An exception to this conclusion is frequently claimed by an appeal to the thief on the cross, Luke 23:39-43. The contention: If the thief was saved without being baptized, why not all of us today?

2. Why not appeal to Abraham on the same ground? to Jacob? to Moses? to David? "But," it is replied, "they were under a different law." So was the thief; he lived and died under the Old Covenant. The New Covenant did not become effective until the death of Him who made it, Heb. 9:15-17.

3. While on earth Jesus had power to forgive sins as He saw fit, Matt. 9:1-8. We are under the covenant of His blood and must comply with its terms, Matt. 26:28; Acts 2:38, 39.

THE SABBATH AND THE LORD'S DAY

The terms "Saturday" and "Sunday" are both of human origin—mere calendar words—and do not affect the Bible issue. We are interested only in what the New Testament says about the first day of the week and worship required of Christians on that day.

In this lesson we propose to show that the Jewish Sabbath was done away in Christ, and that Christians worship on the first day of the week.

I. THE BIBLE AND THE SEVENTH-DAY SABBATH

1. The covenant which included the Sabbath commandment was made with Israel only, Ex. 20:2; Deut. 5:2, 3.

2. Israel was commanded to keep the Sabbath because they had been delivered from the serfdom of Egypt, Deut. 5:15.

3. In giving them the Sabbath, God used the same day upon which He had rested or ceased the work of creation, Gen. 2:3; Ex. 20:8-11; 31:17; Deut. 5:15.

4. The Sabbath was not given or made known until the giving of the law at Mt. Sinai, Ex. 20:10; Neh. 9:13, 14.

5. The Sabbath was a sign between God and the children of Israel, not all nations, Ex. 31:12-17; Ezek. 20:12, 30.

6. The Old Covenant made with Israel when they came out of Egypt, which included the Ten Commandments, Mal.

4:4; 1 Kings 8:9, 21; Deut, 4:13; 9:11, should be abrogated and superseded by the New Covenant, Jer. 31:31-34; Heb. 8:6-13; 10:9.

7. The law of "the handwriting of ordinances" was "nailed to the cross," and the Sabbath, therefore, is no longer binding upon even the Jews, Col 2:14-16.

8. Hosea, the prophet, declared the Sabbath, with all other Jewish observances, would cease when the Gentiles should become the people of God, Hosea 2:11, 23.

9. The apostle Paul declared the Sabbath, with all other Jewish observances, did cease at the cross, Col. 2:14-16.

10. Christians are said to be delivered from the law containing the Ten Commandments, Rom. 3:19; 6:14; 7:4, 6, 7.

11. Those who would be justified by the law given at Sinai are severed from Christ and fallen from grace, Gal. 4:24-31; 5:1, 4.

II. THE BIBLE AND THE FIRST-DAY OF THE WEEK

1. Jesus Christ arose from the dead on the first day of the week, Mark 16:1-9; Luke 24:1, 13, 21, 46.

2. On the first day of the week He was thus declared to be the Son of God, Rom 1:3, 4.

3. Between His resurrection and ascension, Jesus met with His disciples on the first day of the week (several times), John 20:1, 19, 26.

4. Pentecost came on the first day of the week, Lev. 23:15. Hence, all of the events of Acts 2:1-47 took place on the first day of the week.

5. The Holy Spirit came upon the apostles on the first day of the week and began His mission of conversion, Acts 2:1-4, 38.

6. The first gospel sermon proclaiming Jesus as the Christ was preached on the first day of the week, Acts 2:22-36.

7. Three thousand souls, the first fruits of the gospel harvest (Lev. 23:17), were added to the church which began on that Pentecost, the first day of the week, Acts 2:41-47.

8. The church assembled on the first day of the week to break bread and to worship God, Acts 20:7; 2:42; 1 Cor. 16:2; 1 Cor. 11:23, 33; Heb. 10:25.

9. In the New Testament we have the following new things: (1) a New Covenant, Heb. 8:6; (2) a new institution, the church; (3) a new set of ordinances, commandments, 1 Cor. 11:2; 1 Cor. 14:37; (4) a new feast, the Lord's supper; (5) a new day, the first day of the week; (6) a new word to express the new day, *kuriake hemera*, "Lord's day," (Rev. 1:10), a word which was never used before.

10. Yet, in the face of all these New Testament facts, modern Sabbatarians will cling to the seventh-day Sabbath and seek to bind its observance upon Christians.

The seventh-day Sabbath was to Jews only and is done away in Christ. The first day is the Lord's day and is given to Christians. Let us rejoice and be glad in it, Ps. 118:22-24.

PRAYER

There is a universal tendency to pray, recognized among all races in all ages. Solomon's prayer at the dedication of the Temple takes for granted that any stranger who should come from anywhere on earth is likely to be a praying man, 2 Chron. 6:32, 33. As set forth in his sermon on Mars Hill, Paul recognized this universal tendency, Acts 17:22-29.

In this brief outline it is proposed that we consider what prayer is, whose prayer God hears, and something of what man can pray for.

I. WHAT PRAYER IS

1. Prayer is man talking with God. It is the heart's desire, expressed to God, Rom 10:1 . Compare Peter's prayer, Matt. 14:30, and that of the publican, Luke 18:13.

2. Prayer is (1) supplication, an earnest entreaty; (2) petition, wishing toward or alongside one, (3) intercession, an interview on behalf of another; (4) thanksgiving, giving of thanks. See 1 Tim. 2:1, 2.

3. Prayer should not be a memorized speech; it should be spontaneous, from the heart, the outgrowth of fellowship and intimacy with God, "Our Father," Matt. 6:9-15, 7:7-12.

II. WHOSE PRAYER GOD HEARS

1. The basis of prayer is a right relationship with God. This relationship is a Father-son relationship, "Our Father," Matt. 6:9. Only the child of God can address Him as Father.

2. The basis of this Father-son relationship is Jesus Christ, John 14:6, which is established by His blood, Heb. 2:9-11; Eph. 2:14-19.

3. This relationship is sustained by a continuous fellowship with God through Christ in worship and the doing of His will, John 9:31, by abiding in Him, and His word abiding in us, John 15:7.

4. Therefore, God hears,

    (1) the righteous, Jas. 5:16; 1 Pet. 3:12;

    (2) the obedient, 1 John 3:22,

    (3) thosewho lifted up "holy hands,"1 Tim. 2:8;

    (4) His children who do His will, Matt. 6:9; John 9:31.

III. PRAYING IN THE NAME OF JESUS CHRIST

1. Three times in His last discourse with the disciples Jesus emphasized praying in His name, John 14:13, 14; 15:16; 16:24, 26.

2. To ask in the name of Jesus is more than a mere talisman tacked to the beginning or end of a prayer. It is praying "in Him," with His endorsement, backed by all that He is, and as the claimant of all the blessings He has procured. His name:

    (1) Lord: king over all, Rev. 17:14; Phil. 2:9-11.

    (2) Jesus: "savior," Matt. 1:21.

    (3) Christ: "anointed," Acts 2:36; 4:27; Priest and King, Heb. 7:1-4.

IV. AS PRAYER PERTAINS TO THE CHRISTIAN

1. The Christian should pray "always," Luke 18:1; "without ceasing,"1 Thess. 5:17; "steadfastly," Rom. 12:12; "at all seasons," Eph. 6:18.

2. He should pray about all things (not necessarily "for" all things), with thanksgiving for all things, Phil 4:4-7;1 Thess. 5:16-18. An analysis of the prayer Jesus taught the disciples (Matt. 6:8-15) discloses that of the things prayed for, five were spiritual and one was material. It requested only the necessities of life for one day.

3. He should pray for the rulers of his and all lands, 1 Tim. 2:1-7.

4. He should pray for strength in temptation, Matt. 26:41; 6:13.

5. He should pray for all the saints, for the preachers of the gospel and for the triumph and victory of the word in the lives of hearers, Eph. 6:18, 19; Col. 4:2-4; 2 Thess. 3:1, 2.

6. One thing for which he may not pray, "sin unto death," 1 John 5:16, 17 (see Heb. 6:4-6; 10:29-31).

7. The folly of "death-bed repentance," Prov. 1:24-33.

8. When prayer seems unanswered, let not the Christian be discouraged. The prayer may have been contrary to faith, to the will of God, in violation of God's natural or spiritual laws, or God may have something better than that for which he prayed.

V. CONCLUSION

It is recommended that the individual or class make a study of prayer in the life of Jesus and from the epistles of Paul. The life will be enriched by such a study.

THE CHRISTIAN LIFE

The Christian system divides itself into three parts: the doctrine, the worship and the moral life. The life includes blessings, privileges and obligations. Christian character and fellowship with God the result toward which the doctrine and worship were aimed.

This lesson concerns itself with the life of the Christian. Everyone who obeys the gospel is to grow in the likeness of Christ and toward the perfection of God.

I. THE CHRISTIAN LIFE IS A LIFE OF FAITH AND TRUST

1. The Christian is justified by faith, Rom 5:1, 2; walks by faith, 2 Cor. 5:7; lives by faith, Heb. 10:37-39; is guarded through faith, 1 Pet. 1:5; and receives, as the end of his faith, the salvation of his soul, 1 Pet. 1:9.

2. His hope and trust are in God, 1 Tim. 4:10; 6:17; 2 Cor. 1:9, 10.

II. THE CHRISTIAN LIFE IS A LIFE OF BLESSING AND PRIVILEGE

1. The blessing and privilege of sonship, 1 John 3:1-3; involves heirship with Christ, Rom. 8:14-17; Gal. 4:4-7.

2. As a son, whose faith is in his Father, the Christian enjoys the privilege of prayer and petition to God, Matt. 6:9; 7:7-12; Phil. 4:4-7; 1 Thess. 5:16-18; 1 Pet. 3:12.

3. He has the assurance of God's continued care and presence, which enable him to face life with a sure, calm confidence, Heb. 13:5, 6; Jas. 4:7, 8; 1 Pet. 5:7, 8.

III. AS A CHILD OF GOD, THE CHRISTIAN'S LIFE MUST BE ONE OF HOLINESS AND RIGHT CONDUCT

1 . The child of God is to be an imitator of God, Eph. 5:1, 2, an imitation realized in following the steps of Christ, John 8:12; 1 Pet. 2:21, 22. God is his standard of perfection, Matt. 5:48, of holiness, 1 Pet. 1:15, of purity, 1 John 3:3. A high and perfect standard, indeed!

2. He is sanctified, set apart, as a vessel to God's honor, 1 Cor. 1:1, 2; Heb. 12:14; Eph. 5:22-28.

3. His body is a temple of the Holy Spirit, 1 Cor. 6:19, 20; 2 Cor. 6:16-18. As such, he is to perfect holiness in flesh and spirit, 2 Cor. 7:1.

IV. SUCH AN IDEAL IS ATTAINED BY CRUCIFIXION OF THE FLESH, FOLLOWING AFTER THE SPIRIT

1. The Christian has been born again; he has become a new creature, John 3:3-5; 2 Cor. 5:17.

2. He must now put to death the deeds of the body, the old practices, and put on a new character, Col 3:5-17.

3. There must be a crucifying of the flesh and its deeds, Gal. 2:20; 5:24; 6:14.

4. Christ must dwell in the heart by faith, Eph. 3:14-19; Col. 1:26, 27.

V. EMPHASIS MUST BE PLACED UPON A COMPLETE CHANGE OF HEART

1. Jesus placed the emphasis on the heart, the seat of conduct. He goes back to the origin of the act:

(l) "Kill—angry,"Matt. 5:21-26.
(2) "Adultery—lust," Matt. 5:27-30.
(3) "Forswear—swear now not at all," Matt. 5:33.
(4) "Eye... tooth—other cheek," Matt. 5:38-42.
(5) "Love...hate—love your enemies," Matt. 5:43-48.
(6) "Whatsoever ye would—even so do ye,"Matt. 7:12.
(7) Doers—not simply hearers, Matt. 7:21-27.

2. In everything Jesus seeks conduct from the heart, the result of a changed heart, Matt. 12:33-36; 15:7-9, 18-20.

CONCLUSION: Such a disposition is not developed in a day, nor a month; it is a growth, the result of continual pruning, crucifying, developing. It is of such a life that Jesus was speaking when He said, "Enter by the narrow gate . . . few there be that find it," Matt. 7:13, 14.

The Christian life is lived by heavenly principles and for another world, but it is practical, the only practical life in this world.

KEEPING SAVED: DANGER OF APOSTASY

Having shown in the last lesson what it means to be a Christian, in this one we propose to show the importance of keeping saved, of continuing in the Christian life, and that a child of God can apostatize, "fall from grace."

It is argued by some that the child of God, a person once saved, cannot so sin as to be lost. The doctrine is false; it originated with Satan in the garden of Eden when he told Eve she would "not surely die." Let not the child of God be deceived today. Children of God can "fall from grace."

I. THE GRACE OF GOD

1. Grace is "good will, loving kindness, favor" It is favor unmerited by the individual upon whom it is bestowed.

2. God's provision for man's redemption is an expression of His grace, favor, Eph. 2:1-10; Titus 2:11-14; 3:4, 5.

3. God's grace has further provided for man's need as a Christian that he may continue in his saved condition, 1 Cor. 10:13; 1 John 2:1, 2.

4. But in order to continue in the grace of God one must abide in His word, and the word must abide in him, John 8:31, 32; 15:4-10; 1 John 2:24-28.

5. When man ceases to conform to the will of God, he ceases to be in harmony with God; this is what is meant by apostasy or falling from grace.

6. The question of apostasy is not one of will, i.e. what the child of God will do; but it is a question of can—can a child of God so sin as to be separated from God and lost?

II. THE BIBLE TEACHES THAT CHILDREN OF GOD CAN SIN AND BE LOST

1. Israel—claimed by Jehovah as His children, Deut. 14:1, was declared by Paul to have fallen, the record of which is for our admonition, 1 Cor. 10:1-13. Paul also recognized the possibility of his own apostasy, 1 Cor. 9:24-27.

2. Saul—God's Spirit was upon him, 1 Sam. 10:6-10, but God became his enemy, 1 Sam. 28:16. Saul killed himself, 1 Sam. 31:4, 5. Do murderers go to heaven? 1 John 3:15.

3. The vine and the branches, John 15:1-10. There can be no branch apart from a vine, so there can be no child of God or branch apart from Christ. But those in Christ are children of God, Gal. 3:26; 4:7. But branches, some of those in Christ, were cast out and burned. A child of God can be lost.

4. The kingdom—Only the children of God are in the kingdom, having been born again, John 3:3-5. But some are cast forth from the kingdom into hell, Matt. 13:47-50; 25:1-13 (five foolish virgins); 25:14-30 (note v. 24, "His own servants . . . his goods," and v. 30, the same servant.

5. The building, 1 Cor. 3:10-17. The builders are Paul and Apollos; the building is the church; the material builded into it are the kinds of persons; the fire is the tests that come to these. Some endure, some are lost; but lost or saved, the builders' destiny is not affected thereby.

6. The "book of life"—Children of God have their names there, Luke 10:20; Phil. 4:3; Heb. 12:23. Those who sin are blotted out, Ex. 32:33. Those not written there, whether never at all or blotted out, are cast into the fire, Rev. 20:15.

7. Christ crucified afresh—When one becomes a Christian, Christ is formed within, Gal. 4:19; Eph. 3:17. Therefore, only the Christian could crucify Him afresh, and this some have done and can do by "falling away," Heb. 6:4-8.

8. Sanctified ones sin willfully, Heb. 10:26-31. These

have no hope, only a fearful expectation of judgment. Note, the ones of whom he writes are those who have been sanctified by the blood of Christ!

9. Back under the law—Those going back under the law fall from grace, Gal. 5:4. Can a child of God return to the law?

10. Those leaving their first love, Rev. 2:4, 5, 7. Those who left their first love, have fallen, are told to repent. The tree of life is promised only to those who repent. What of those who do not overcome?

11. Departing from the faith—Some shall fall away from the faith, 1 Tim. 4:1; men made shipwreck of it, 1 Tim. 1:18; led astray from it, 1 Tim. 6:10, may deny the faith, 1 Tim. 5:8; by false teaching, overthrow the faith of some, 2 Tim. 2:18. This looks like apostasy, does it not?

12. Christians are admonished to make their calling and election sure, 2 Pet. 1:10; believers may be condemned with the world, 1 Cor. 11:29-33 (world already condemned, John 3:18); last state worse than the first, 2 Pet. 2:20-22.

V. CONCLUSION

If the saved man cannot sin, why did God provide a law for the forgiveness of his sin? 1 John 2:1, 2; Acts 8:22; James 5:16, 17. Be faithful and keep saved.

SECOND COMING OF CHRIST

The second coming of the Lord is the great day of all days. In it and that which follows is realized the consummation of the Christian system and the eternal purpose of God. It should be anticipated by Christians with joyous expectation.

About the second coming there is much speculation. Let us get the issue clearly before us. We believe emphatically in the second coming of Christ. The speculations of men we deny. Rutherford taught that He came in 1914. This we deny. Premillennialists teach He is to return, raise the saints for a season of rapture, come on to earth and reign for a thousand years, raise the wicked dead at the end of a little season, then judge. This we also deny. We affirm He is to return, raise the dead—all the dead—judge all, and deliver the kingdom unto God.

I.   THE SECOND COMING OF CHRIST

1. It is necessary for the consummation of the scheme of redemption and purpose of God, Heb. 9:27, 28; Phil. 3:20, 21; 1 John 3:1-3.

2. It is sure. It is backed by the promise of Jesus Himself (see His parables) and is guaranteed by His resurrection, Acts 17:30, 31. It was proclaimed by angels, Acts 1:9-11, and was a cardinal doctrine of the apostles, 1 Thess. 4:16-18; 2 Thess. 1:5-10; Rev. 1:7.

3. The time is completely unknown to man, reserved within the authority of God, Mark 13:32; Matt. 24:27, 36-44; 25:13; Acts 1:7. To set a time or declare it as imminent is pure speculation.

4. The manner is with or on the clouds of heaven, Acts 1:9-11; 1 Thess. 4:16-18; 2 Thess. 1:6-10; Rev. 1:7. He did not come in 1914.

II. THINGS TO BE ACCOMPLISHED AT HIS COMING

1. The resurrection of the dead—all the dead, John 5:28-29; last day, John 6:40, 44, 54; Rev. 20:12, 13; last trump, 1 Cor. 15:51; those afflicted and those afflicting, 2 Thess. 1:5-10.

2. The judgment of men, Matt. 25:31-46; Rev.20:11-15.

3. Glorification of the saints, Col. 3:4; 1 John 3:2; bodies changed, Phil. 3:20, 21; 1 Cor. 15:51, 52.

4. Punishment of the wicked, 2 Thess. 1:7-9; Rev. 1:7.

5. Passing of the present order, and the ushering in of new heavens and a new earth, 2 Pet. 3:4-13.

6. The kingdom shall be delivered up to the Father, 1 Cor. 15:20-28.

III. THE JUDGMENT AND THE JUDGE

1. The judged: all men of all ages, great and small, Rev. 20:11-15; Matt. 25:31-46. None excused, 2 Cor. 5:10; Rom. 14:10-12.

2. The Judge: Jesus Christ, into whose hand God has committed all judgment, John 5:22; Acts 10:42, 43;17:30, 31; 2 Tim. 4:1. He is Son of man and Son of God.

3. The standard of judgment; the word of God, "books," Rev. 20:12. The Jews who lived under the law to be judged by the law, Rom. 2:12; all since Christ to be judged by the gospel, Rom. 2:16; John 12:48.

IV. THE THINGS FOR WHICH WE MUST GIVE ACCOUNT AND BE JUDGED

1. Attitude toward the gospel:

(1) Refusing to hear, Matt. 10:14, 15; Rom. 2:3-6

(2) Refusing to repent. Matt. 11:20-25; 12:38-42.

(3) Refusing to obey, Rom 2:7-11; 1 Pet. 4:17; 18; 2 Thess. 1 :7-10.

2. Thoughts and intents (purposes) of the heart, Eccl. 12:13, 14. Thoughts are the springs of character, disposition, acts and words, Matt. 12:34, 35; 15:18, 19.

(1) The lustful look is adultery, Matt. 5:28.

(2) Hatred is murder, 1 John 3:15.

(3) Covetousness is idolatry, Eph. 5:5.

3. Words, Matt. 12:36, 37. idle words, Eph. 4:29; James 1:26; 3:7-10; lying words, Rev. 21:8, 22:15; profanity, etc.

4. Deeds and works, Matt. 16:27; Eccl. 11:9-11.

V. CONCLUSION

Man's greatest obligation is to "prepare to meet [his] God" The wages of sin is death and destruction but never annihilation, Rom. 6:23; Matt. 25:41, 46.

THE END: ETERNAL LIFE, ETERNAL PUNISHMENT

The language of Isaiah, quoted by Paul as descriptive of the gospel, well describes man's conception of the hereafter: "Things which eye saw not, and ear heard not, and which entered not into the heart of man, whatsoever things God prepared for them that love him" (1 Cor. 2:9). All that he can know is that which God has declared.

In this lesson we propose only a brief outline from which student and teacher may begin a study of this sublime subject.

I. REWARD AND PUNISHMENT ARE ETERNAL

1. Definition. Eternal: *aionios* describes duration, either undefined but not endless, as in Rom. 16:25; 2 Tim. 1:9 Tit. 1:2; or undefined because endless as in Rom. 16:26, and the other sixty-six places in the N.T"—W. E. Vine, *Expository Dictionary of New Testament Words.*.

2. Set in contrast with temporal (literally, "for a season"), 2 Cor. 4:18.

3. It is used of persons and things which are in their nature endless, as, e.g., (1) Of God, Rom 16:26; His power, 1 Tim. 6:16; His glory, 1 Pet. 5:10. (2) Of the Holy Spirit, Heb. 9:14. (3) Of the redemption procured by Christ, Heb. 9:12. (4) Of the life received by those who believe in Christ, John 3:16, "never perish," John 10:28. (5) Of the salvation of the obedi-

ent, Heb. 5:9. (6) Of the resurrection body, 2 Cor. 5:1; "immortal,"1 Cor. 15:53. (7) Of the life, Tit. 1:2, and punishment, 2 Thess. 1:9, finally realized after the judgment, Matt. 25:46. (8) Of the sin that "hath never forgiveness," Mark 3:29. (9) Of the judgment of God, from which there is no appeal, Heb. 6:2. (10) Of the fire of punishment, Gehenna, Mat. 18:8, 9:25:41; Jude 7, "unquenchable," Mark 9:43.

II. HEAVEN

1. The eternal dwelling place of God, Matt. 5:16; 12:50; Rev. 3:12.

2. From there the Son of God descended, John 3:13, 31; 6:38, 42; 7:29.

3. There He ascended, Act 1:9-11; Heb. 4:14; 9:24.

4. He sat down on the right hand of God in heaven, Heb. 8:1; where He now is, 1 Pet. 3:22.

5. From there the Holy Spirit came on Pentecost, Acts 2:33; 1 Pet. 1:12.

6. It is the abode of the angels, Matt. 18:10; 22:30.

7. From there Christ will descend at His return, 1 Thess. 4:16; Phil. 3:20, 21.

8. It is to be the eternal dwelling place of the saints in glory, 2 Cor. 5:1. (For a symbolic description of it, study Rev. 21, 22.)

III. HELL

1. Three words should be studied: *sheol, hades,* and *gehenna. Sheol* (Hebrew) and *hades* (Greek) are equivalents, Psalm 6:10; Acts 2:27, 31, and mean "The unseen world, the state or abode of the dead" (I.S.B.E.). These words are used of the abode of the dead until the resurrection, never of the state or abode after the judgment. At the judgment, death and hades are cast into the lake of fire, Rev. 20:24.

2. *Gehenna* is found twelve times in the New Testament, eleven of these by Jesus. In the American Standard Version it is uniformly translated "hell." It is a transliteration of the Hebrew for valley of Hinnom, a place of refuse where once

children had been burned to Molech, 2 Kings 23:10; and said to have been the burying place of punishment to the Jews, Jer. 7:32.

3. *Gehenna* (hell, A.S.V.) is always used with reference to eternal punishment, Matt. 18:8, 9; Mark 9:47, 48, etc.

IV. THE NATURE OF THE ETERNAL PUNISHMENT IN HELL

1 . Eternal fire:
    (l) a lake, Rev. 19:20; 20:14, 15; 21:8;
    (2) a furnace, Matt. 13:42, 50;
    (3) unquenchable Mark 9:43, 47, 48;
    (4) everlasting, Matt. 25:41;
    (5) prepared for the devil and his angels, Matt. 25:41.
2. Outer darkness, Matt. 22:13; 25:30.
3. Anguish and tribulation, Rom 2:8, 9.
4. Sorer than death without mercy, Heb. 10:28, 29.
5. Torment, day and night forever, Matt. 8:28, 29; Rev. 20:10.

V. CONCLUSION

Between heaven and hell stands every man and woman making a decision, which determines his or her destiny for one or the other.

ENDNOTES

[1] Thayer's *Greek-English Lexicon of the New Testament*, p. 632.

[2] Form in the body of Christ is not confined to organizational structure. God foreordained that Christians are to be conformed to the image of his son (Rom. 8:28-29). This is the spiritual form the church takes. This imagery identifies with Christ when we love each other as he loved us: "By this all men will know that you are my disciples" (John 13:34-35).

[3] It should be noted that the identity of the Lord's church extends to both form and function. Regarding form we think of the universal body of redeemed humanity that is organized into local congregations (e.g., Rom. 16:16; 1 Cor. 1:1; 16:19a; 1 Thess. 1:1), under congregational leadership (e.g., Acts 14:23; 20:17; Phil. 1:1; 1 Tim. 5:17; Heb. 13:17, 24). Regarding function, we think of lovingly caring for others, of individual Christian lifestyles, of worship and evangelism, all characterized by a Christlike love that contributes to the overall identity of our relationship to Christ (John 13:34-35). At the same time, to think biblically, we think of function as embracing corporate worship in the local assembly (1 Cor. 14:23-26; Heb. 10:25), of congregational benevolence (2 Cor. 8-9), of congregational instruction (Acts 13:1) and of congregational evangelism (2 Cor. 11:8; Phil. 4:15-16). But neither form nor function can be accomplished in and by the church without apos-

tolic guidelines (doctrine) that are accepted universally as authoritative (pattern). Thus, the identity of the church, as God would have it, extends to both function and form.

[4] The processes of revelation, by which gospel knowledge was divinely imparted to the apostles and prophets of Christ, and of inspiration, by which the apostles spoke and wrote unerringly, as two separate works of the Holy Spirit are detailed by Paul in 1 Corinthians 2:10-13. God revealed to the apostles so they could know the things of God (1 Cor. 2:10-12) that prior to that revelation were a mystery (1 Cor. 2:6-9). A second function of the Spirit was to guide the apostles to "speak, not in words which man's wisdom teacheth, but in words which the Spirit teacheth" (1 Cor. 2:13). We call that speaking process inspiration.

[5] An attempt to make the language of Hebrews 8:13 say that the Old Covenant was yet in existence at the time of the writing of the Hebrew letter contradicts the language of the text. The point of Hebrews is that the Old Covenant was close to vanishing at the moment Jeremiah prophesied the coming of a New Covenant.

[6] Edward C. Wharton, *Freed for Freedom* (Nashville: 21st Century Publishing Co., 1995).

[7] See, The Church of Christ, Edward C. Wharton, Chapter 3, "The Purpose of Baptism," for documentation.

[8] Only Jesus in his sinless state could "fulfill all righteousness" under the law when he was baptized by John. The legal system of the Mosaic law demanded sinless perfection, condemned the violator at the first infraction and could not justify the sinner. It was necessary for Christ to be baptized according to the commandment which God added to the law in order to be righteous and to become our righteousness, our sinless sin-offering and our high priest.

[9] "Firstborn" is plural, the firstborn *ones*. Not Christ, but the church. This term expresses the idea of the special relationship the firstborn son sustained to the Hebrew family (Deut. 21:15-17). The idea of "firstborn' is one of primacy, of preeminence, which emphasizes the special relationship of

Christians to the Father.

[10] The study of the nature, form, function, and resulting identity of the church does not complete the study of the gospel. This study is not an exposition of the saving love and mercy of God through the cross of Christ. But keep in mind that while we are saved by a person rather than by a doctrine, we must obey the doctrine from the heart in order for that person to save us. For an exposition in 13 lessons on salvation by grace through faith in Christ, see Edward C. Wharton, *Freed for Freedom* (Nashville: 21st Century Christian, 1995).

[11] See what Jesus said in Matthew 15:6-9 about the substitution of human traditions for the commandments of God.

[12] William Hendriksen, *Gospel According to Matthew* (Grand Rapids: Baker Book House, 1973), p. 1001; R.C.H. Lenski, *St. Matthew's Gospel* (Wartburg Press), p. 1175.

[13] Stephen L. Caiger, *Archaeology and the New Testament* (London: Cassell and Co., 1948), p. 164; Adolph Deissmann, *Light from the Ancient East* (New York: George H. Doran Co., 1927), p. 121; Adolph Deissmann, *Biblical Studies* (Edinburgh: T. and T. Clark, 1909), pp. 146-47; George Milligan, *The Vocabulary of the Greek New Testament* (Grand Rapids: Wm. B. Eerdmans, 1954), p. 451; quotation from James D. Bales, *The Case of Cornelius* (Delight, Ark.: Gospel Light Pub. Co., 1964), p. 84.

[14] Hendriksen, p. 1000.

[15] W.E. Vine, *Expository Dictionary of New Testament Words* (Revell), p. 97.

[16] Myron S. Augsburger, *Matthew*, The Communicator's Commentary (Word Publishing), p. 331.

[17] Bales, pp. 83-84.

[18] Neil Lightfoot, "Notes on Selected Passages in 1 Corinthians," *Restoration Quarterly*, Vol. 3, No. 4, 1959, p. 175.

[19] David Prior, *The Message of 1 Corinthians* (Inter-Varsity Press), p. 37.

[20] F.W. Grosheide, *Commentary on the First Epistle to the Corinthians* (Grand Rapids: Wm. B. Eerdmans), p. 39.

[21] William Barclay, *The Letters to the Corinthians*, The Daily Bible Study (Edinburgh: The Saint Andrew Press), p. 18.

[22] Bales, pp. 84-85.

[23] The idea that baptism into the name of Christ merely symbolizes that we have already become the Lord's possession is contrary to every definition we have seen placed upon the phrase.

[24] We must use caution not to draw conclusions from Scripture analogies that are not inherent in those analogies. Romans 6:1-4 does not say the alien sinner dies to sin at repentance and is then, as a dead man, buried in baptism. Paul does not say that. He says that the sinner dies to sin when buried with Christ at baptism.

[25] While denominationalism is religious division, mere division in the body of Christ, as in 1 Corinthians 1:10-12, is not to be equated with denominationalism. Denominationalism is more than mere religious division. A denomination is not the church inasmuch as denominations do not teach God's revealed plan of salvation by faith in Christ, repentance from sins and baptism for the remission of sins. The church is the saved body of Christ. Sinners must believe and obey the Lord's teaching for salvation before they can constitute the church. Until a denomination teaches the New Testament's teaching for salvation it cannot be a part of the saved body of Christ.

[26] Paul referred to the unsaved as "alien" sinners, as those outside of covenant relationship with God, and therefore were not privileged citizens in the kingdom of God (Eph. 2:11-19).

[27] The New King James Version speaks of the church as coming into existence on Pentecost after Christ's resurrection (Acts 2:47).

[28] Daniel 7:14 foresees the Messiah "given dominion and glory and a kingdom." "Kingdom" is variously translated "sovereign power" (NIV) and "sovereignty" (marginal rendering of the NASB). So also in Daniel 7:27a.

[29] George Campbell, James Macknight and Philip Doddridge render it, "Indeed, I say to you, some of those who are present, shall not taste death, until they see the Son of Man

enter upon his Reign." In Matthew 12:28; Luke 10:11; 17:20-21; John 3:3, Romans 14:17 and others, *basileia* is rendered "reign" instead of "kingdom." A translation of the New Testament with prefaces, emendations, and appendix by Alexander Campbell, 6th edition (Pittsburgh: Forrester & Campbell, 1839).

[30] The sovereign reign of Christ was powerfully manifested not only in the destruction of Jerusalem, wherein some confine the fulfillment of Matthew 16:28 and Mark 9:1, but also in his bestowal of power to establish his church. By this means the reign of Christ was not only announced (Acts 2:30-36) but also confirmed (Acts 2:43).

[31] Hades is the place of disembodied spirits. The Scripture seems to say conclusively that all the spirits of mankind, both righteous and unrighteous, go to the hadean world immediately after death. Luke 16:19-31; 23:43; Acts 2:22-31 will explain that while the rich man went to "torments" in Hades, Jesus and the thief went to "paradise" in Hades. At the final day, death or the grave, where the body is, and Hades, where the spirit is, will give up the dead in them to the bodily resurrection (Rev. 1:18; 20:11-15).

[32] This does not teach that the church will always exist somewhere on the earth. It is not inherent in this prophecy of Christ to claim that if the church does not always exist at some place in the earth, Hades has prevailed against the church. The prophecy that Hades shall not prevail against the church is not speaking of the church in history, but of the church at the end of history at the resurrection.

[33] Most translations have God agreeing with the apostles: "and whatsoever you (the apostles) bind on earth shall be bound in heaven." But Jesus has the apostles agreeing with God. Thus, the ultimate authority is God.

[34] It is sometimes claimed that the John 14:26 and 16:13 Scriptures were Christ's promise to the church that the Holy Spirit would guide Christians into the truth. But the promise is given only to the apostles. If the Holy Spirit were presently revealing to the church, she would not need the New

Testament. Also, in keeping with the promise in John 14:26, the Spirit would remind the apostles of what Jesus had said during his ministry. But the church today cannot be reminded of what she has not heard Jesus say.

[35] God's purpose for man's redemption was a mystery from before the foundation of the world to Pentecost. But the Holy Spirit revealed the mystery to the apostles. Since the mystery has been revealed, there is no new truth needed to be revealed. Before Paul wrote 1 Corinthians, all truth had already been revealed by the Spirit to the apostles (1 Cor. 2:10-12). He and the rest of the apostles preached the words given by the Spirit (1 Cor. 2:13) that our faith, created by that word, might be in Christ and not in the wisdom of men (1 Cor. 2:1-5). This was the order by which the apostles received the mind of Christ (1 Cor. 2:15-16). Spiritual men receive the mind of Christ from the apostles (1 Cor. 2:14); carnal men do not.

[36] They were not to test the prophets, but the spirits of the prophets, that is, the source of the prophets' teaching. All gospel truth came by revelation through the Holy Spirit (1 Cor. 2:6-10). All teachings to the contrary come from "the spirit of the world" (as indicated in 1 Cor. 2:12). Hence, John's exhortation to "test the spirits whether they are of God."

[37] Thayer, p. 243.

[38] Ethelbert Bullinger, *Lexicon and Concordance*, p. 566.

[39] Here, as elsewhere, consistency would ask for it to be translated "shepherd."

[40] William Barclay, *The Letters to Timothy, Titus, Philemon*, The Daily Bible Study (Edinburgh: The Saint Andrew Press, 1964), p. 113.

[41] William Ramsay, *The Teaching of Saint Paul in Terms of the Present Day* (Grand Rapids: Baker Book House, Reprinted in 1979), p. 41.

[42] William Ramsay, *Pauline and Other Studies in Early Christian History* (New York: Gordon Press, 1977), p. 67.

[43] Barclay, *Timothy*, p. 113.

[44] *The Interpreter's Bible*, Vol. XI, p. 451; Irenaeus, *Against Heresies* II, 22; W.M. Ramsay, *Historical Commentary*

on the First Epistle to Timothy; The Expositor, Ser. 7, Vol. 9, p. 237, and *The Cities and Bishoprics of Phrygia.*

[45] *Word Studies in the Greek New Testament,* p. 1036.

[46] F. F. Bruce observes, "There was in apostolic times no distinction between elders (presbyters) and bishops such as we find from the second century onwards: the leaders of the Ephesian church are indiscriminately described as elders, bishops (i.e. superintendents) and shepherds (or pastors)." *Commentary on the Book of Acts* (Grand Rapids: Wm. B. Eerdmans Pub. Co., 1966) , p. 415.

[47] The language of Titus 1:5 does not suggest that there can be one eldership over all the churches of Christ in a given city. Elders are not appointed over a city, but over each church *in* a city. Titus was to appoint elders in every city where there was a church.

[48] F. W. Mattox, *The Eternal Kingdom* (Delight, Ark: Gospel Light Pub. Co., 1961), pp. 107-111.

[49] Peter's first epistle is not addressed to a local church but to a large segment of the body of Christ in Pontus, Galatia, Cappadocia, Asia and Bithynia (1 Peter 1:1). Hence, 1 Peter is called a general epistle.

[50] Earl D. Radmacher, *What the Church Is All About* (Chicago: Moody Press, 1972), p. 348.

[51] Character: moral and spiritual qualities. Capabilities: his ability to superintend a diversified group of people, his expertise to oversee, spiritually shepherd and otherwise "take care of the church of God." Proper motivation: he desires the oversight for the spiritual and eternal benefit of the church, not for the monetary gain or authority he might exploit from such perquisites that may be invested in the ministry.

[52] The Revised Standard Version's rendering, "married only once" is without justification. The word "once" is not in this context. It is more of an interpretation than a translation. The RSV footnote qualifies its rendering by adding, "Greek *the husband of one wife.*" This amounts to an admission that the RSV rendering is more of an interpretation than a translation. A rather literal translation would be "a one wife kind of

man." There is nothing in the New Testament that indicates an elder could not have had a prior marriage as long as the dissolution of that marriage and the state of his present marriage are not in violation of any other teaching of Scripture.

[53] Thayer, p. 138.

[54] Vine, pp. 272-73.

[55] These Hellenists were Grecian Jews who had come from outside Palestine to the feast of Pentecost. They had become believers while in Jerusalem and had not yet returned home. They were descendents of the Israelites who centuries earlier had been deported into Assyrian and Babylonian captivities. Though Israelites they were reared in a Gentile environment and probably could not speak Hebrew (cf. Acts 2:5-11). The traditional Palestinian Israelites were apparently not sympathetic to the Gentileness of these Hellenists.

[56] Thayer, p. 257.

[57] Vine, p. 202.

[58] Thayer, p. 346.

[59] Thayer, p. 346.

[60] Vine, p. 67.

[61] Ibid., p. 69.

[62] The King James Version renders this, "in whom also we have obtained an inheritance." But the better translation seems to be "in whom also we were made a heritage" (ASV). The idea is not what we obtain, but what we become, a heritage for God.

[63] Francis A. Schaeffer, *The Church at the End of the Twentieth Century* (Downers Grove, Ill.: Inter-Varsity Press, 1970), p. 59.

[64] Ibid., p. 61.

[65] Ibid., p. 62.

[66] Ibid., p. 63.

[67] Henry Clarence Thiessen, *Introductory Lectures in Systematic Theology*, p. 410.

[68] Radmacher, p. 317. At the time of this writing (1972) Radmacher was president of Western Conservative Baptist Seminary.

[69] A prophet speaks for God by the inspiration of the Holy Spirit; therefore, an inspired teacher would be a prophet. But Paul makes a distinction between prophets and teachers.

[70] Vine, pp. 235-36

[71] The Greek translation of the Hebrew Old Testament.

[72] Vine, p. 236.

[73] From *sebomai*, a word that means to revere and stresses the feeling of awe or devotion is translated "worship" in Matthew 15:9. Jesus exposes the hypocrisy and unacceptability of those whose worship follows the doctrines of men instead of the worship that is according to God's Word.

[74] Vine, p. 236.

[75] Ibid., p. 215.

[76] *The Living Bible.*

[77] The condemnation of Amos (5:21-24; 6:1-6) was not of the instruments of music in the old covenant worship anymore than he condemned lying upon beds of ivory or of eating lambs out of the flock or of anointing themselves with oil. Their sacrifices were not acceptable because their lives were not acceptable. They were idolatrous and immoral. Their worship was therefore a farce. The prophet's condemnation was against mere perfunctory ritualism in the midst of luxury and insensitivity "for the affliction of Joseph."

SELECTED BIBLIOGRAPHY

Arndt, and Gingrich. *A Greek-English Lexicon of the New Testament.* The University of Chicago Press, 1957.

Bales, James D. *The Case of Cornelius.* Delight, AR: Gospel Light Pub. Co., 1964.

_____, *The Deacon and His Work.* Shreveport, LA: Lambert Book House, 1967.

Barclay, William. *The Letters to Timothy, Titus, Philemon.* Edinburgh: The Saint Andrew Press, 1964.

Bruce, F. F. *Paul, Apostle of the Heart Set Free.* William B. Eerdmans Publishing, 1977.

_____, *New Testament History.* Garden City, NY: Day, 1972.

_____, *The Book of the Acts.* The New International Commentary on the New Testament, Grand Rapids: Wm. B. Eerdmans Pub. Co., 1966.

Cloer, Eddie. *What Is the Church?* Searcy, Ark.: Resource Publications, 1993.

Deason, Larry. *The Love of Christ in the Local Congregation.* Clifton Park, NY: Life Communications, 1993.

Ferguson, Everett. *Backgrounds of Early Christianity.* Grand Rapids: Wm. B. Eerdmans Pub. Co., 1990.

_____, *Early Christians Speak.* Abilene, TX: ACU Press, 1987.

Flew, R. Newton. *Jesus and His Church.* London: Camelot Press, 1960.

Hailey, Homer. *From Creation to the Day of Eternity.* Las Vegas: Nevada Publications, 1982.

Hawley, Roger. *Redigging the Wells.* Abilene, TX: Quality Publications, 1976.

Jividen, Jimmy. *Worship in Song.* Ft. Worth, TX: Star Bible Publications, 1987.

Kuen, Alfred F. *I Will Build My Church.* Chicago: Moody Press, 1971.

McGuiggen, Jim. *The Reign of God.* Lubbock, TX: Montex Publishing Co., 1979.

Mattox, F. W. *The Eternal Kingdom.* Delight, AR: Gospel Light Publishing, 1961.

Moore, John, and Ken Neff. *A New Testament Blueprint for the Church.* Chicago: Moody Press, 1985.

Murch, James DeForest. *The Free Church.* Louisville: Restoration Press, 1966.

_____. *Christians Only.* Cincinnati: Standard Publishing Co., 1962.

Radmacher, Earl D. *What the Church Is All About.* Chicago: Moody Press, 1972.

Ramsay, William M. *Pauline and Other Studies in Early Christian History.* New York: Gordon Press, 1977.

_____. *The Teaching of St. Paul in Terms of the Present Day*. Grand Rapids: Baker Book House, reprinted 1979.

Schaeffer, Francis A. *The Church at the End of the 20th Century*. Downers Grove, IL.: Inter-Varsity Press, 1970.

Smith, F. LaGard. *The Cultural Church*. Nashville: 20th Century Christian, 1992.

Thayer, Joseph A. *Thayer's Greek-English Lexicon of the New Testament*. Peabody, Mass.: Hendrickson, reprint 1995.

Vine, W. E., *Expository Dictionary of New Testament Words*. Los Angeles: Fleming H. Revell Co., 1959.

Walker, Richard. *The Kingdom*. Livingston, TN: Gary and Winnie Worley, 1996.

Wharton, Edward C. *Freed for Freedom*. Nashville: 21st Century Publishing Co., 1995.